Reading Aids Series

# Prereading Activities for Content Area Reading and Learning

## Second Edition

David W. Moore
*University of Northern Iowa*

John E. Readence
*Louisiana State University*

Robert J. Rickelman
*Millersville University*

An **ira** Service Bulletin

International Reading Association
Newark, Delaware 19714

# INTERNATIONAL READING ASSOCIATION

Copyright 1989 by the
International Reading Association, Inc.

**Library of Congress Cataloging in Publication Data**

Moore, David W.
  Prereading activities for content area reading and learning/
David W. Moore, John E. Readence, Robert J. Rickelman. 2nd ed. p.c.m.
(Reading aids series) Bibliography: p.
  1. Reading readiness. 2. Content area reading. I. Readence, John E., 1947- . II. Rickelman, Robert J.  III. Title.  IV. Series. V. Series: IRA service bulletin.
LB1050.43.M66          1989  428.4'07–dc19 88-23140 CIP
ISBN 0-87207-233-9

Staff editor: Romayne McElhaney
Cover design: Boni Nash
Cover photo: Mary Loewenstein-Anderson

# Contents

# Foreword

Prereading preparation—no instructional concept in content area reading is more sensible or powerful. Involving students in text material that may be remote and abstract, if not deadly dull, is no easy matter. The authors of this second edition of *Prereading Activities for Content Area Reading and Learning* offer us a wealth of prereading activities and strategies designed to make unfamiliar, uninteresting material accessible to maturing readers.

Preparing students to read content area material can be easily neglected in a classroom teacher's march to cover the content. Yet the payoffs associated with prereading activities are considerable. Readers not only learn to bring to the text what they know already about the topic under study; they also approach what they read confidently, with anticipation and purpose. Showing students that they know more than they think they do about the material to be encountered during reading is what prereading instruction is all about.

I commend David Moore, John Readence, and Robert Rickelman for the revisions and extensions they have made in this second edition. You will find the chapters well-organized around several important aspects of prereading instruction. Each chapter is packed with practical suggestions that are theoretically sound. I am particularly impressed with the connections the authors make between writing and reading in the chapter entitled "Writing before Reading."

As you approach this volume ask yourself, "What do I know already about prereading activities?" Make a list, jotting down those things that come to mind immediately. Now turn to the Contents page, peruse the chapter titles, and then reflect on the question, "What do I need to learn more about?" Prereading activities, such as the one you just participated in, are rooted in the principles of cognitive readiness. If you are ready to approach this volume, I invite you to begin your reading—and enjoy!

Richard T. Vacca
Kent State University

# Preface

**P**rereading *Activities for Content Area Reading and Learning,* second edition, matches the first edition in that it describes numerous ways to prepare students to learn from printed materials. It is a compendium of activities, or teaching strategies, that teachers can employ. Examples are provided along with the descriptions of most activities. The activities are grounded on the principle that prereading preparation is essential for maximum learning.

This second edition differs from the first in several ways. A major new thrust emphasizes students' independence, and learning strategies instruction is characterized by fading from teacher centered demonstrations to student centered applications. Several chapters describe strategies for teaching students to manipulate factors that affect their learning. A second major change is the inclusion of a chapter on writing. Although most of the teaching activities in both editions capitalize to some degree on writing, a separate chapter is included to keep pace with the rapidly expanding knowledge about the role of writing in learning from text.

A minor change in the format of the chapters was made in this edition. Each chapter contains a statement of purpose and, with the exception of Chapter 1, a list of the teaching strategies described. Some new teaching strategies are included, and information from the earlier edition's first and last chapters are combined. The writing style continues to be informal.

As with the first edition, this monograph is meant to be a practical guide to activities that are applicable in busy classroom situations.

DWM

JER

RJR

The International Reading Association attempts, through its publications, to provide a forum for a wide spectrum of opinions on reading. This policy permits divergent viewpoints without assuming the endorsement of the Association.

# Preparing Students to Read in the Content Areas

**Purpose**    *Chapter 1 introduces the remaining five chapters of this monograph. The first section comments on lesson planning. It describes the importance of connecting prereading and postreading activities and presents the stages of individual lessons as well as a program of lessons. The second section describes five factors affecting learning which teachers can address during prereading activities.*

Content areas such as biology, history, and vocational arts present distinctive viewpoints and explanations of the world. Reading materials used during the study of these subjects often contain unfamiliar concepts, strange terms, and unusual styles of writing. Consequently, students frequently require guidance.

Guiding students is the opposite of simply handing out a passage and telling students to read it and be ready to discuss it. Guidance means providing activities before, during, and after students read a passage in order to help them understand and retain what they encounter.

This monograph emphasizes prereading guidance — what to do before students read a passage. Teachers present students with ideas they will encounter and encourage an active search for meaning. Some of the talk that typically occurs after reading a passage is moved forward. Students are prepared for their assignments during the prereading stage.

The value of activities that prepare students for reading has been recognized in the professional literature for almost a century. For instance, Herbart (1898) stimulated attention to this aspect of lesson planning. He noted that in the preparation stage of a reading lesson, "The object is to give the thoughts of the pupil a definite tendency, to arouse expectation, stimulate interest, and give intellectual activity from the beginning."

As you read this monograph, keep in mind that subject matter teachers have at least two aims of instruction: to teach students information about the world and to teach students strategies for learning about the world on their own. To quote a popular aphorism: "Give me a fish and I eat for a day. Teach me to fish and I eat for a lifetime." This monograph presents techniques teachers can use to fulfill these aims of instruction.

## Reading Lessons

To clarify your thinking as you read this monograph, think of reading lessons in two ways: individual reading lessons and a program of reading lessons. Individual lessons take place in a day or two and involve a single reading passage; a program of lessons takes weeks, months, or even years to complete and involves numerous reading passages. Individual lessons and programs of lessons are separate but related topics. A feature they share is that they can be divided into stages.

### Individual Lessons

Individual lessons have before, during, and after stages. Teachers prepare students in the prereading, before stage; offer help in the during reading stage; and follow up the reading in the postreading, after stage. Practically every lesson described here engages students before, during, and after they read.

A crucial aspect of individual lesson planning is that students need to review what they read just as they need to be prepared for what they read. Even though this monograph emphasizes prereading activities, review and enrichment after reading are essential for maximum learning. Review allows students to refine their reactions to what they read.

This publication describes postreading followups that are connected closely with initial prereading activities. If students are directed to read in order to learn how General Custer was defeated at the Little Big Horn, then after reading the students should reflect on how Custer was defeated. The value of prereading preparation is lost if there is no review or if the postreading activities ignore what the students were prepared to accomplish. Reading lessons contain stages that should be connected.

### A Program of Lessons

A program of lessons is a systematic progression of individual lessons, a long term series of activities focused on a certain goal. In this monograph, independence is the goal. The program of lessons described is intended to teach students independent strategies for learning from text—one of the aims of instruction. Individual lessons emphasize information about the world, and the program of lessons emphasizes independent learning strategies. By following a coherent program of lessons, teachers can develop students' performance with strategies such as predicting and organizing information.

A program of lessons that has received much notice is direct instruction (Rosenshine & Stevens, 1986). Direct instruction carries many labels and descriptions, although it most frequently is said to consist of three overlapping stages. The terms we use are *demonstration, guided practice,* and *independent application.*

Teachers begin the demonstration stage as the dominant figure in the class, then they begin fading out their role so students become the dominant figures as they independently apply the strategies they have been taught. Demonstration calls for teachers to explain a learning strategy (such as outlining), tell when it should be used, and describe why it is useful. Teachers then model the strategy, thinking through the process aloud as they perform it. The next step is to provide guided practice.

The guided practice stage of direct instruction involves repeated exercises, feedback, and possible reteaching. After demonstrating how to construct an outline, teachers instruct their students to read a passage and outline it. Having students explain their outlines to others helps clarify the strategy. After outlines are completed, students might compare theirs with the teacher's or with other students'. Frequent opportunities to construct outlines and receive feedback should be offered during this stage.

Independent application is meant to help students become automatic with the strategy being taught and to integrate it into their repertoires. Clear demonstrations and extensive guided practice sessions are prerequisites for successful independent applications. Teachers should allow class time for students to apply outlining. Schedule a quiz for the end of a class and allow students to use their outlines. Teachers might record a weekly grade for students who outlined particular passages. The thrust of these independent application activities is to provide relevant situations for students to use what has been presented.

To summarize, a program of lessons is needed to teach students independent learning strategies, and direct instruction is such a program. When following this approach, teachers dominate the lessons during the initial demonstration stage, teachers and students provide equal input during the guided practice stage, and students dominate during the independent application stage.

## Factors That Affect Learning

Prereading guidance emphasizes five factors that affect learning from text: expected learning outcomes, motivation, content knowledge, attention, and learning strategies. Teachers can manipulate these factors to promote students' learning about the world during individual lessons, and students can manipulate these factors independently through a program of lessons. If appropriate learning outcomes are expected and made known, if students are motivated to learn, if their content knowledge is sufficient, if they know what information deserves attention, and if they apply appropriate learning strategies, then learning from text can be expected. The remainder of this chapter explains how these five factors affect learning from text.

## Expected Learning Outcomes

Outcomes are the concepts, principles, attitudes, and strategies students are expected to acquire from their study of a particular subject. One way expected outcomes affect learning is by defining what is acceptable. If expected outcomes are too high, students and teachers will believe little has been learned; if expected outcomes are too low, students and teachers will falsely believe much has been learned. Students and teachers need to share expectations of what constitutes acceptable learning so students' progress can be monitored appropriately.

To determine expected learning outcomes for a certain piece of text, consider what it offers in relation to the learning outcomes expected for the course. Read a passage and ask, "What should my students learn from this?" One way to determine what students should learn is to consult the school district's curriculum guide. In the absence of such a guide, read an upcoming passage, close the book, and jot down what you expect students to acquire.

It is difficult to determine reasonable expectations about what students should learn from a passage. One difficulty is the diversity of possible learning outcomes. For instance, teachers might expect students to learn new vocabulary ("What is a covalent bond?"), follow text organization ("Summarize this chapter."), or generate personal examples ("Provide examples of the statement, 'Power corrupts'.") Teachers also expect students to emerge from reading with improved learning strategies as well as new information.

A second difficulty in determining reasonable expectations is that content area specialists often believe information is stated directly in a text when, in fact, it is only mentioned indirectly. This occurs because content area teachers know their discipline so well that the mere mention of a concept triggers their knowledge of that concept. Unfortunately, mere mention of a concept might trigger practically nothing in students' minds. For instance, a science text might mention that Darwin's theory of evolution changed people's view of the world as fundamentally as did Copernicus' theory of the universe. This information might convey to a specialist a clear perspective on Darwin, but expecting students to understand it might be unreasonable. Given the relative value of information for different people, teachers need to read materials with a student's perspective to determine reasonable learning outcomes.

In brief, expected learning outcomes affect teachers' and students' learning from text. Teachers need to study a passage and decide what part students reasonably can be expected to learn. When making this decision, teachers need to consider the clarity with which texts present particular information.

# Motivation

Along with expected learning outcomes, the motivation readers have relative to a passage influences learning. Since motivation sustains a person's behavior, providing motivation is an essential task for content area teachers. Ideally, all students are highly motivated, eager learners with the urge to master new information. Realistically, many students are frustrated, apathetic learners who view reading assignments as something to avoid. Before guiding students through content materials, teachers frequently need to convince students to begin the journey. Students who will not read are as disadvantaged as students who cannot read.

Teachers motivate their students by guaranteeing success, providing clear feedback, and maintaining a positive outlook. Enhancing students' self-esteem on a long term basis goes far in developing motivation. Curiosity is another determinant of motivation (Ball, 1982). Young children, adolescents, and adults want to explore their environments. When presented with a new stimulus, they want to know about it. This natural phenomenon drives people to seek information. People like to make sense of what often appears to be an uncertain, chaotic world. Capitalizing on students' curiosity is a motivational strategy that can be addressed readily during prereading activities.

To determine what motivation is needed to guide students to expected learning outcomes, assess the motivational value of the reading materials. Some materials engage readers' curiosity by the nature of topics presented or with devices such as visuals, problems to be solved, and anecdotes that connect information with students' lives. Other materials provide lifeless information. Similarly, some students are eager to learn; others are indifferent. If motivation is a concern, teachers can look to the prereading activities described in this monograph — Directed Reading-Thinking Activity, List-Group-Label, and Guided Writing Procedure — as partial solutions. Prereading activities tend to motivate students by stimulating their curiosity about the contents of a passage.

# Content Knowledge

Assuming that reasonable learning outcomes are set and students are motivated to read, successful learning depends largely on students' prior knowledge of the content (Anderson & Pearson, 1984). Two important aspects of students' content knowledge are amount of knowledge and activation of knowledge.

*Amount of knowledge.* Already knowing a lot about what is on a page promotes learning. To appreciate this point, read the following paragraph and retell it in your own words.

> Two experiments investigated visual processing asymmetries in normal and dyslexic readers, with unilateral tachistoscopic presentations. The experiments employed randomized or blocked presentations of verbal and nonverbal materials to determine whether previously reported differences between dyslexics and normals

were due to structural hemispheric differences or to strategical processing differences. The results indicate that if dyslexics are unable to predict the nature of the stimulus, they behave as normal readers. Their atypical laterality emerges only when they can adopt a strategy in anticipation of a specific type of stimulus (Underwood & Boot, 1986, p. 219).

Could you retell this passage in your own words? You probably were motivated enough to read it carefully, and you knew the expected outcome, but we suspect your learning was incomplete due to limited content knowledge.

In order to understand the sample paragraph, prior knowledge is needed about visual processing asymmetries, unilateral tachistoscopic presentations, and randomized or blocked presentations. Readers need to know these specific terms and have a general idea about the type of research being conducted. If you did not know much about what the paragraph reported, your learning was impaired.

Some materials present concepts that are more familiar than others. Some science books present *erosion* and *tides;* others present *heliozoans* and *interoceptors*. The differences in clarity of presentation also can be surprising. Well written materials explain ideas various ways. If *condensation* were to be introduced, a well written science text would define it by stating that in condensation a gas or vapor loses heat, decreases in volume, and turns into a solid or liquid. The text would illustrate products of condensation such as sweat on glasses of ice water, clouds, rain, snow, and frost. Condensation might be contrasted with evaporation, and the base word, *dense,* might be highlighted. The natural tendency for matter to contract when it becomes cold could be stated. Conversely, a poorly written text might introduce condensation by stating that it involves uniting molecules to form new, heavier, and more complex compounds.

In order to plan effective content reading lessons, examine the familiarity of the passage contents. Determine the amount of content knowledge students require in order to achieve expected learning outcomes. The gap between what your students already know and what the passage presents helps determine what teachers need to provide during the prereading stage of an assignment.

*Activation of content knowledge.* For maximum learning, students need prior knowledge about the topic being studied and they need to relate that prior knowledge to the contents of the passage (Anderson, 1985). To appreciate this point, read the following:

> The procedure is actually quite simple. First you arrange items into different groups. Of course one pile may be sufficient depending on how much there is to do. If you have to go somewhere else due to lack of facilities that is the next step; otherwise, you are pretty well set. It is important not to overdo things. That is, it is better to do too few things at once than too many. In the short run this may not seem important but complications can easily arise. A mistake can be expensive as well. At first, the whole procedure will seem complicated. Soon, however, it will become just another facet of life. It is difficult to foresee any end to the necessity for this task in the immediate future, but then, one never can tell. After the procedure is

completed one arranges the materials into different groups again. Then they can be put into their appropriate places. Eventually they will be used once more and the whole cycle will then have to be repeated. However, that is part of life (Bransford & Johnson, 1972, p. 722).

You may have thought this paragraph was incomprehensible. Individual sentences made sense, but the paragraph did not seem to hang together. If you were to retell everything you could remember about the paragraph, your score probably would be quite low. However, if you had known before reading the passage that it was about washing clothes, you would have thought it comprehensible.

As demonstrated, knowing about the contents of a passage is important, but such knowledge is useless if it is not related to the contents of the passage being studied. Knowing something about washing clothes is important for understanding the sample paragraph; knowing that the passage is about washing clothes is equally important. Activating learners' content knowledge before reading a passage is an important prereading activity.

Students may know a lot about various content area topics but may not activate what they know. Having content knowledge and activating content knowledge are related but separate concerns. If reading materials fail to demonstrate how new concepts fit with what students already know, then prereading activities might be needed.

It is important to realize that the activities included in this monograph focus more on activating prior knowledge than on developing it. These activities involve oral or pencil and paper tasks; they help activate what students already know. Additional teaching probably will be needed if students have little knowledge of the subject. Direct experiences with concrete objects, pictures, filmstrips, guest speakers, experiments, and field trips might be needed in order to develop students' content knowledge.

## Attention

Learners have a limited capacity for absorbing and making sense of information. This becomes readily apparent when two persons talk to you at the same time. You must internally turn off one message and listen only to the other or you will be overwhelmed and miss both messages. Because of limited capacities, readers need to attend to the important information in a passage and disregard what is trivial. Otherwise, all words, phrases, sentences, and paragraphs appear worth learning, and the barrage of information is overwhelming. Efficient readers direct their attention to the important ideas (Anderson & Pearson, 1984). Focusing attention deserves time during prereading activities along with determining expected learning outcomes, motivating students, and developing and activating content knowledge.

The reader or the writer can determine what deserves attention. Readers' purposes for reading and writers' presentations of information regulate readers' attention (van Dijk, 1979). To illustrate, think of skimming a history text for a particular date to use in a report. The writer might have mentioned the date only one time because it was considered to be of minor importance, but the reader might consider the date to be the crucial aspect of the passage. For another example, read the following paragraph.

Native Americans
The biggest differences that developed among the Native Americans were a result of where they settled to live. There were five main living centers where these people settled: the Northwest Coast, the California region, the Southwest, the Eastern woodlands, and the Plains.

Some readers might decide that the important information in the paragraph is what caused the biggest differences among Native Americans; others might think the number of main living centers deserves emphasis; still others might focus on locations of living centers. Moreover, one might read only to determine if the Southeast were considered a main living center of Native Americans, and another might study the passage to determine if it is well written. All five or none of these purposes could constitute acceptable reasons for reading. Readers' purposes for reading influence the aspects of a passage that deserve attention.

Although readers frequently let their specific reasons for reading regulate their attention, they also allow writers to regulate their attention. Rather than search for specific information, readers often study a passage to learn what the author emphasized and thus considered important.

Writers accentuate important information several ways, and textbook writers rely quite heavily on adjunct aids. Adjunct aids consist of parts of texts such as the questions and activities inserted in a chapter; typographical marks such as boldfaced headings, subheadings, and marked words; pictorial aids such as pictures, illustrations, diagrams, maps, tables, and graphs; glossaries and footnotes; and introductions and summaries. These pieces of text are adjunct because they either highlight or complete the meaning of the main body of the text. They are designed to lead readers to the important information in the text.

Many current textbooks contain adjunct aids. The questions and activities encourage students to go beyond the information given in the text, and the pictorial aids supplement textual information. Teachers should examine these aids to see whether the writer emphasized information that fits their curriculum.

Attention affects what is learned from text. During the prereading stage of reading lessons, teachers decide whether they should help students focus their attention on pertinent information or have students focus without help. In addition, teachers and students decide whether the students' purposes for reading or the writer's presentation of ideas should direct attention.

## Learning Strategies

Reasonable learning outcomes might be expected during a lesson. Students might have appropriate levels of motivation, their content knowledge might be sufficient and active, and their attention might be directed to information, but they still could have difficulty understanding and remembering text information because of their learning strategies.

Learning strategies (a term practically synonymous with study skills) are tactics employed to achieve certain goals. Many strategies have been identified through the years (Laycock & Russell, 1941; Weinstein & Mayer, 1986). Visualizing information, rereading troublesome parts of a passage, reviewing information frequently, and creating mnemonic devices are a few learning strategies. Three powerful strategies that can be incorporated readily into prereading lessons are predicting, connecting, and organizing (Moore et al., 1986).

*Predicting.* Predicting involves anticipating the information in a passage and calls for readers to think ahead while reading. Once readers have a set of expectations for a passage, they can read and see which expectations are met, which are not, and what unexpected information is encountered. Students who do not predict upcoming information generally are unprepared for the stream of ideas they encounter.

Helping students predict information is an essential feature of the prereading teaching strategies presented in the remaining chapters of this monograph. The Survey Technique, PReP, Contextual Redefinition, Webbing, and Free Writing all provide students an advance idea of the contents of upcoming passages. These teaching strategies help students predict the contents of passages written about diverse topics. In addition, they can be converted to learning strategies by having students assume responsibility for previewing passages and forming predictions.

*Connecting.* Perhaps the best way to learn new information is to connect it to prior knowledge. Connecting involves relating what is being presented to what is already known; linking new information to old is the essence of the connect learning strategy. To illustrate, think back to the *Native Americans* passage in this chapter. You might connect the information in that passage with what you already know by thinking of specific tribes that live in the five main centers. "I know about the Apache, Navajo, and Pueblo Indians in the Southwest, and I know their traditional way of life differs from the Sioux and Comanche Indians of the Plains." Remembering the principle that environment influences life helps explain why differences are found among American Indians.

Connecting information enhances learning. New concepts are fitted into a network of preexisting concepts, thereby holding the information in place and providing access to it. Teaching strategies that promote prediction also promote connections. For instance, Webbing and Free Writing encourage students to assimilate new information with the old.

*Organizing.* Organizing information is another powerful learning strategy. Students who arrange ideas according to meaningful classifications have an advantage over those who do not. Part of organizing information involves following the pattern of ideas presented by an author. Readers who are sensitive to an author's writing patterns typically learn more than readers who are insensitive to the patterns. Thus, it seems worthwhile to help students determine whether passages are written according to a pattern such as time sequence, simple listing, or problem solution. The Survey Technique and Outlining presented in this monograph are prereading strategies that emphasize the organization of passages.

Another part of organizing information involves assimilating ideas according to readers' prior knowledge. This aspect of organizing is quite similar to connecting information. To illustrate, animal life can be studied according to body systems such as respiration, musculature, and reproduction. Once students know the organization of body systems, that structure can be used when studying new life forms. Students could organize information about any animal's body system regardless of the writer's presentation. In a sense, students' minds have a set of labeled slots to fill. Webbing and Graphic Organizing are two strategies that capitalize on organizing information according to students' prior knowledge.

## Summary

Two aspects of reading lessons were described in the beginning of this chapter. First, individual reading lessons consist of three stages—before, during, and after—that should be connected. Individual reading lessons include activities that prepare students for a passage, guide them during their reading, and follow up after the reading. Preparation is of little use if it is not connected with the postreading task. Second, a program of lessons consists of a series of activities directed toward some goal. Direct instruction—consisting of demonstration, guided practice, and independent application—is one approach to developing learners' independent strategies.

The second section of this chapter described five factors that affect learning from text: expected learning outcomes, motivation, content knowledge, attention, and learning strategies. It is important to realize that all five factors can be addressed during the prereading stage of individual lessons to promote learning from text, and students can be taught to manipulate these factors independently through a program of lessons.

### References

Anderson, R.C. Role of the reader's schema in comprehension, learning, and memory. In H. Singer and R.B. Ruddell (Eds.), *Theoretical models and processes of reading,* third edition. Newark, DE: International Reading Association, 1985.

Anderson, R.C., and Pearson, P.D. A schema-theoretic view of basic processes in reading comprehension. In P.D. Pearson (Ed.), *Handbook of reading research.* New York: Longman, 1984, 255-291.

Ball, S. Motivation. In H.E. Mitzel (Ed.), *Encyclopedia of educational research,* fifth edition. New York: The Free Press, 1982, 1256-1263.

Bransford, J.D., and Johnson, M.K. Contextual prerequisites for understanding: Some investigations of comprehension and recall. *Journal of Verbal Learning and Verbal Behavior,* 1972, *11,* 717-726.

Herbart, J. *The application of psychology to the science of education.* B.C. Mulliner, Editor and Translator. London: Swan Sonnenschein, 1898.

Laycock, S.R., and Russell, D.H. An analysis of thirty-eight how to study manuals. *School Review,* 1941, *49,* 370-379.

Moore, D.W., Moore, S.A., Cunningham, P.M., and Cunningham, J.W. *Developing readers and writers in the content areas.* New York: Longman, 1986.

Rosenshine, B., and Stevens, R. Teaching functions. In M.C. Wittrock (Ed.), *Handbook of research on teaching,* third edition. New York: Macmillan, 1986, 376-391.

Underwood, G., and Boot, D. Hemispheric asymmetries in developmental dyslexia: Cerebral structure or attentional strategies? *Journal of Reading Behavior,* 1986, *18,* 219-228.

van Dijk, T.A. Relevance assignment in discourse comprehension. *Discourse Processes,* 1979, *2,* 113-126.

Weinstein, C.E., and Mayer, R.E. The teaching of learning strategies. In M.C. Wittrock (Ed.), *Handbook of research on teaching,* third edition. New York: Macmillan, 1986, 315-327.

Chapter 2

# Asking and Answering Questions
# before Reading

**Purpose** *This chapter demonstrates the effective use of questions to guide students' learning and prescribes a set of teaching and learning strategies designed to allow students to assume responsibility for asking their own questions of texts in independent learning situations.*

**Strategies** 1. *Question-Answer Relationships* helps students answer comprehension questions more efficiently by analyzing the task demands of various types of questions.

2. The *Directed Reading Activity* uses teacher questions to activate prior knowledge, create interest, and establish purposes for reading.

3. The *ReQuest* procedure helps students formulate their own questions about text they are reading and develop effective questioning behavior.

4. The *Directed Reading-Thinking Activity* provides guided practice for students setting their own purposes for reading.

5. The *Directed Inquiry Activity* uses six key questions – Who? What? When? Where? Why? How? – to encourage students to make predictions about a text to be read.

6. The *Survey Technique* helps students preview a text and independently formulate their own purposes for reading.

$Q$uestions play an integral part in learning about the world. It is difficult to imagine attempting to function effectively without asking questions and receiving answers. Questions also play a dominant role in reading and learning from text (Klauer, 1984), and they are a major tool in the instructional repertoire of teachers.

The questioning strategies included here are designed to stimulate students' curiosity about a passage to be read, activate prior content knowledge, lead students to anticipate and elaborate what they read, and focus attention on important information. The expected learning outcome is that students will use questions to set their own purposes for reading text material. In addition, the strategies to be discussed demonstrate a progression from teacher demonstration and modeling of effective questioning (using the DRA), to student guided practice in using effective questioning (using ReQuest, DRTA, and DIA), to independent student questioning (using the Survey Technique). This progression is intended to lead students from dependent to independent learning from text.

## Levels of Processing

Before proceeding to a discussion of specific teaching strategies, one important aspect of questioning should be considered—the level of understanding of the the text by students. Pearson and Johnson's (1978) levels of processing construct focuses on this aspect of questioning. It provides a framework for developing questions that help students use their own thoughts and prior experiences to interact with the information provided by a text. As such, the levels of processing construct might be a tool to help teachers lead students beyond merely parroting an author's words.

Pearson and Johnson proposed three levels of text processing: text explicit, text implicit, and experience based. These levels correspond to three levels of comprehension proposed by Herber (1978): literal, interpretive, and applied. *Text explicit* processing involves getting the facts as stated in a text. A text explicit question is explicitly cued by the language of the text. Readers can point to the answer in the text, and there is only one correct answer. *Text implicit* processing, on the other hand, requires readers to determine an appropriate answer drawn from the text and from their prior knowledge. Text implicit questions are based on the language of the text, but require readers to derive an answer not directly visible in the text. Readers are asked to infer what the text implicitly states and elaborate the given information. Readers take the facts presented in the text and add knowledge from their own experiential backgrounds to derive a plausible answer implied by the author. Answers may vary depending on the type of experiences readers bring to the text, but the answers must be consistent with the information stated in the text. Finally, experience based processing requires readers to think beyond what is stated in the text. When experience based questions are asked, readers must draw information from their prior knowledge to derive plausible answers. Answers to these questions are based mainly on reader experience as they are not obtained directly from the text, making possible numerous answers.

A paragraph with accompanying questions to illustrate the levels of processing follows.

### The Quest

As Tom peered through the thick undergrowth, he could barely make out the figure that stared back at him. Cautious not to let the heat of the sun confuse his judgment, he trudged closer to the figure to identify it more accurately.

1. What was Tom peering through?
2. Where was Tom?
3. What else might Tom have done after seeing the figure?

In question 1, the answer comes directly from the text—*thick undergrowth*. In question 2, the answer is not directly visible. Thus, the facts of *thick undergrowth, heat of the sun,* and *trudged* might be added with prior knowledge to answer *jungle, woods,* or *savanna*. All of these answers are plausible interpretations given the language of the text and the different backgrounds of readers. Finally, in question 3, many answers would be allowable as they are not derived from the text but from readers' experiences.

## Concerns about Questioning

There are a number of concerns about teacher originated questions used to enhance students' reading and learning. First, formulating good questions representative of all levels of processing requires time and thought. Second, questions must provide specific cues for students' comprehension. General, diffuse questions might not facilitate comprehension; questions should provide the cues needed for students to respond. Third, what you ask about is what students learn (Wixson, 1983). For example, students who read to find answers explicitly stated in a text tend to learn only that information. This technique may be helpful when the text is especially dense. On the other hand, students who read to answer higher level questions that call for text implicit or experience based processing tend to acquire more overall information from a text.

Finally, students who have learned to depend on teachers to ask questions may not learn to ask appropriate questions of themselves. Fillion (1981) reported that students are conditioned to respond rather than to initiate. He pointed out that teacher questions (1) are not necessarily the questions students would ask or want to have answered, (2) crowd out students' opportunities to ask questions, and (3) do not permit us to find out whether students are learning to ask questions on their own. In other words, answering questions only indirectly teaches the skills necessary for independent reading (Readence & Moore, 1979).

## Question-Answer Relationships

Students should be proficient in answering questions before we ask them to generate their own. The Question-Answer Relationships (QARs) strategy (Raphael, 1984) can help students learn to answer questions appropriately.

The QARs help students identify responses to questions. Using a modification of Pearson and Johnson's (1978) levels of processing construct, Raphael (1984, 1986) suggested teaching students to use the three processing levels, relabeled for ease of understanding. Her terminology for the three levels and the mnemonics used for each are: right there (text explicit) — words used to create the question and words used for the answer are in the same sentence; think and search (text implicit) — the answer is in the text, but words used in the question and those in the answer are not in the same sentence; and on my own (experience based) — the answer is not found in the text.

Teaching students to use QARs is based on four instructional principles: give immediate feedback; progress from shorter to longer texts; begin with simple questions and progress to complex questions; and, develop independence by beginning with group learning exercises and progressing to individual, independent activities.

Raphael suggested teaching QARs in three stages. In stage one, consisting of four parts, QARs are introduced and practice is given at identifying task demands while answering questions. Short paragraphs are used with one question from each of the QAR categories accompanying them. Instruction proceeds from most support to least support. Students are given (1) the text, question, answer, QAR label, and reason why the label is appropriate; (2) the same information with instructions to generate their own reason for the appropriateness of the QAR label (immediate feedback is given to students on the accuracy and completeness of their reasoning); (3) the text, question, and answer with the request to supply the label and their reasoning; and (4) the text and question with students expected to supply the rest.

In stage two, students work through longer texts containing more questions. The teacher guides groups of students through an initial QAR as a review. Then, students work through remaining exercises while the teacher provides feedback individually on QAR selection and answer accuracy.

In stage three, a chapter or a full story is broken into four segments, each followed by six questions — two per QAR category. The first segment is a review done individually but corrected as a group. The remaining three segments are completed individually with appropriate individual feedback. Since text selections do not necessarily support all types of questions, two questions per category are only a guide for teachers and students.

Using QARs allows students to independently analyze a text question and derive an appropriate answer. Once students gain independence in answering questions, teachers can teach them how to ask good questions. With QAR as a basis, we will describe a series of instructional strategies we believe will move students from dependence on the teacher to independence in asking their own questions as they read.

## Directed Reading Activity

The Directed Reading Activity (DRA) is a teaching strategy developed by Betts (1946) as a comprehensive means of guiding students through a text selection. Although there are a number of stages in the complete DRA strategy (see Tierney, Readence, & Dishner, 1985, for a discussion of the entire procedure), our central concern is the prereading, or readiness, stage of the lesson.

The prereading stage involves activating students' prior knowledge related to the text selection, creating motivation to read it, and setting the purpose for reading. Questions can play an important role in preparing students to read the text.

Teachers can ask text implicit or experience based questions to engage students' prior knowledge and stimulate their interest in the text. Even more crucial is asking a question that will guide students through the entire text selection. If a specific reason is not given for reading, students may treat all information as equally important and attempt to master it all. Teachers' overall concern in designing a purpose setting question should be what they want students to know after they read the text. Once this is determined, teachers should focus students' attention on important information throughout the entire passage by asking an appropriate question. Thus, demonstration is one function of teacher questioning in the prereading stage of the DRA. Students can be expected to learn what effective questioning is.

The following sample text will be used as an example of the type of questions teachers might ask students before they read. This sample may not be typical of the length of text students may be assigned to read in their classes; it is being used for illustrative purposes.

### Light from the Sun

The white light of the sun is made of red, orange, yellow, green, blue, and violet all mixed together. At noon when you look toward the sun, the sky looks white because you see all the colors at once. When you look upward away from the sun, the sky looks blue. The sunlight comes through a thin layer of air containing fine dust and water droplets. These small particles scatter the white light into its colors, but only the blue light comes down to earth.

At sunset, the sky often looks red. When the sun is low, its light must pass through more dust filled air than when it is overhead. In the air close to the earth, dust particles are larger than they are in the upper air. These coarse particles scatter all colors except the reds. They give the sky a crimson glow.

Twenty miles above the earth, the air is very thin. Here the sky has no color at all. Even though the sun never sets in space, a day in space is blacker than our night. There is no daylight, for what we call that by name on earth is made up of thousands of reflections. However, even though space is black, we can see to read in it. A book, like the specks of dust or droplets of water in the earth's atmosphere, would reflect the light always streaming from the sun (adapted from Branley, 1963).

Since teachers will decide what specific information deserves attention, let's assume that students will be expected to learn the following, listed in order of importance.

1. What we see on earth in daylight is caused by reflected light from the sun.
2. Even though outer space lacks daylight, we can see objects because of reflected light.

In asking questions about this text, teachers will attempt to activate students' prior knowledge about light from the sun and thus create interest in reading the text. Some students may lack sufficient knowledge to deal with these questions. However, the questions are intended to generate discussion and to find out what knowledge students possess. Since students have not read the text, the following questions might be asked.

1. What color is sunlight?
2. Why is the sky blue during the day and sometimes red at sunset?
3. Why can we see things during daylight?
4. What color is outer space?

These are representative of the kind of questions teachers should ask to activate prior knowledge and generate interest. Also, these questions enable teachers to introduce the material to be read and prime students for a purpose setting question. Next, teachers might ask students the following questions to focus their attention on the major concepts when they do read the text.

5. Can you read a book if you are closed in a dark closet? Why or why not?
6. Can you read a book in the darkness of outer space?

By asking questions 5 and 6, teachers set students up for the purpose setting question they need to answer as they read the text.

7. Why is it possible to read in outer space even though daylight does not exist there?

Such a question should increase students' anticipation of the text to be read and give teachers an opportunity to demonstrate the higher order question necessary to guide students through an assigned text.

## Guided Practice in Student Questioning

While teacher questions are of value in reading and learning from text, it is important for students to be able to generate their own questions in order to become independent learners. Promoting active comprehension through self-questioning (Singer, 1978) helps students toward such independence.

The object of active comprehension is to provide students with practice in question asking and to guide their thinking in learning from text before, during, and after reading. Singer and Donlan (1982) and Wong (1985) provide evidence that student generated questions can lead to improved comprehension. They feel that generating questions entails a deeper processing of the text because students become more motivated and actively involved in the comprehension process.

Singer (1978) proposes that the key to active comprehension is to guide instruction so skill in asking questions will transfer from teachers to students. He suggests a three stage model designed to teach for transfer of question asking: (1) modeling, (2) phase out/phase in strategies, and (3) active comprehension. Modeling is teachers showing students what constitutes good questioning behaviors. This entails taking students through lessons, demonstrating the kinds of questions to ask, and modeling the processes of thinking involved in designing questions. Phase out/phase in strategies (guided practice) occur when students are encouraged to progress through lessons that involve teacher guidance and provide a safe atmosphere in which students can ask questions in their efforts to comprehend the text. Gradually, teachers withdraw. As students begin to ask their own questions without teacher prompting, they are engaging in active comprehension (independent application).

Using Singer's three stage model, we can see the teacher originated questions in the DRA as a means by which to demonstrate effective question asking behavior for students. Next, students are provided an environment that stimulates phase out/phase in strategies. Finally, strategies follow that focus on independent application and active comprehension. Our discussion of asking questions before reading follows this plan.

## ReQuest

ReQuest, an acronym for *reciprocal questioning*, is a strategy developed by Manzo (1969) to help students (1) formulate their own questions about the text they are reading, (2) develop an active inquiring attitude toward reading, (3) acquire purposes for their reading, and (4) develop independent comprehension abilities. ReQuest involves students and teacher silently reading portions of text and taking turns asking and answering questions concerning that material. It is the reciprocal nature of the questioning sequence that differentiates ReQuest from teacher directed questioning strategies and provides the format for students' active involvement. Palincsar and Brown (1984) have shown that training in reciprocal questioning, in conjunction with use of other comprehension fostering activities, can promote students' comprehension of text.

The role of the teacher is central to the success of this strategy. The teacher answers students' questions and serves as a model by asking thought provoking questions that extend students' developing concepts. As such, ReQuest can be conceived of as a phase out/phase in strategy in the Singer model. Teachers continue to demonstrate good questioning behaviors, and students gradually assume more responsibility in the questioning sequence as they become accustomed to the strategy. Thus, ReQuest helps bridge the gap between teachers' modeling question asking behavior for students and active comprehension through use of students' own questions. The ReQuest technique consists of

- Preparing the text
- Readying the students
- Developing questioning behaviors
- Developing predictive behaviors
- Reading silently
- Discussing the reading

In preparing the text for ReQuest, teachers must assure that its difficulty level is suitable for the students and decide how much material will be read at one time (one sentence, one paragraph, etc.). The ability and maturity levels of the students dictate the amount of text to be read. Finally, teachers identify appropriate points in the text where predictions will be elicited.

To provide an example of some aspects of ReQuest, a portion of our previously used sample passage, *Light from the Sun,* has been reproduced. For the sake of illustration, we will assume the passage is at the appropriate difficulty level and that it has been decided to read only one sentence at a time. Two points (designated $P_1$ and $P_2$) have been identified where it has been decided to elicit predictions from the students about the passage.

### Light from the Sun

The white light of the sun is made of red, orange, yellow, green, blue, and violet all mixed together. At noon when you look toward the sun, the sky looks white because you see all the colors at once.[P1] When you look upward away from the sun, the sky looks blue. The sunlight comes through a thin layer of air containing fine dust and water droplets.[P2] These small particles scatter the white light into its colors, but only the blue light comes down to earth.

Prepare the students by giving them the guidelines for ReQuest. It also may be necessary to acquaint students with any new vocabulary in the text and to create interest or develop background for the reading. Having students read the title and tell you what they know about the topic would suffice in many cases.

Following silent reading, students ask questions of the teacher. The teacher answers the questions and, in turn, refines and extends the developing concepts by asking questions of students. For instance, after reading sentence one of our sample text, the teacher should ask "What colors are in white?" so students are able to generalize the notion that white is made up of many colors.

Similarly, after reading sentence two, ask students "If white light comes from the sun, why do you think the sky around it is only blue?" To reemphasize, the reciprocal nature of questioning in this technique is what differentiates ReQuest from more traditional questioning strategies.

When a sufficient amount of the text has been read, predictions about the outcome of the selection are elicited from the students. Students also must provide justifications for their predictions. In the case of our sample text, it was decided to ask for predictions early ($P_1$) because the topic is straightforward and the leading question would lead to predicting the content. The second prediction point ($P_2$) was chosen as a backup just in case students were unable to generate predictions at $P_1$.

Once predictions are generated, justified, and discussed, students silently read the rest of the text to verify their predictions. After the reading, discussion of the text ensues with the prime focus being the reconsideration of the students' predictions about the outcome of the selection.

By formulating their own questions about a text and trying to construct questions to extend the teacher's thinking, students become actively involved in the comprehension process before they read the material. Eliciting student predictions serves as the culmination of this prereading strategy as it leads students to tie together what they know in order to formulate those predictions. Students then read with greater readiness as they attempt to verify their predictions.

When ReQuest is first used, students ask many text explicit questions. It is here that teachers ask questions on higher levels of comprehension to act as a model and to help students integrate the text material they are reading with their prior knowledge of the topic. Thus, the teacher can be assured that students will be introduced to the major concepts to be learned from the text. Simultaneously, teachers are beginning the phase out/phase in strategy of active comprehension. Through the reciprocal nature of ReQuest, students gradually learn to ask thought provoking questions as question asking responsibility shifts to them through repeated experiences with the strategy. This transfer may be further promoted by QAR training, and by having students work in pairs or small groups, without teacher guidance, and asking questions of one another using the procedural steps of ReQuest.

Perhaps a greater impetus to students' independent question asking ability would be to have them take a more dominant role in asking questions about a text and in purpose setting. The next two strategies described, the Directed Reading Thinking Activity and the Directed Inquiry Activity, attempt to provide students such an opportunity.

## Directed Reading-Thinking Activity

The Directed Reading-Thinking Activity (DRTA), developed by Stauffer (1969), enables students to take a more dominant role in preparing themselves to read a text as teachers become moderators. The DRTA is based on the notion that students will develop their abilities to predict, connect, and organize text information while they read and will continually refine their purposes as they use their prior knowledge to understand the text. The DRTA begins with the generation of hypotheses for reading and continues with the refinement of these hypotheses as new information is extracted from text. In essence, the reader poses questions, tests these questions while reading the text, generates new questions, and modifies previous predictions as reading progresses.

The DRTA consists of (1) directing the reading thinking process and (2) fundamental skill training. The first entails setting purposes for reading, reading to verify those purposes, pausing to evaluate understanding, and then proceeding to read with the new purposes. The second consists of students reexamining the text to learn to effectively use reading skills such as word attack, contextual analysis, and concept development. The focus of the discussion is on the initial phase of the DRTA—directing students' reading thinking behaviors to promote active comprehension.

Essentially, directing the reading thinking behaviors of students involves three steps: predicting, reading, and proving. Teachers should divide the text to be read into appropriate segments. Students proceed through a segment of text to define purposes for reading and to evaluate and revise these purposes using the information they acquire. Teachers act as facilitators of this process.

Using our *Light from the Sun* example, students are directed to read the title, examine any accompanying pictures or diagrams, and make predictions as to the content of the text selection. They are encouraged to offer different suggestions and to critically evaluate these suggestions. Students are then directed to read a segment of text to check their predictions. It should be noted that vocabulary is not introduced prior to reading; therefore, students should be encouraged to utilize the context to figure out unknown words they encounter.

After they have read the initial segment, students are directed to close their texts, and an examination of the evidence ensues. Previous predictions about the content are evaluated in light of new information. Students are asked to provide proof of their predictions and text segments may be read orally for verification. If evidence causes students to refine their predictions, new predictions are generated. Students then are directed to read a new segment of text, and the predicting, reading, and proving cycles continue. As reading progresses, predictions, which at first may be divergent, generally will converge as more information is amassed. Once predictions about the text converge, students are directed to read the rest of the selection on their own.

The DRTA goes beyond the reciprocal give and take of ReQuest. Teachers withdraw their demonstration of effective questioning behavior and provide guided practice for students as they formulate their own purpose setting questions about the text.

## Directed Inquiry Activity

Thomas (1986) suggests that the Directed Inquiry Activity (DIA), a modification of the DRTA, be used when students encounter content text containing an abundance of factual material, much of which is to be retained by the reader. The format of the DIA retains the essential purposes and many of the features of the DRTA, but differs by utilizing a framework of six key questions: Who? What? When? Where? Why? How?

Like the DRTA, the DIA begins with an initial survey of the title, subheadings, and accompanying pictorial material. Students are encouraged to predict responses to the six key questions with predictions recorded and expanded wherever possible. When predictions are terminated, students are directed to read the rest of the material to verify their predictions. Following this, a critical analysis of the predictions is undertaken, using information gained from the reading. If necessary, modifications are made under appropriate points of inquiry. The DIA attempts to promote active comprehension on the part of students who are now asked to initiate rather than only respond to questions.

## Survey Technique

Our final strategy of this chapter, the Survey Technique (Aukerman, 1972), is a whole class adaptation of the initial step of the SQ3R study method. Students systematically analyze the various graphic aids present in a text reading assignment and use their prior knowledge to formulate purposes for reading. This prereading strategy consists of

- Analyzing the chapter title
- Analyzing the subtitles
- Analyzing the visual aids
- Reading the introductory paragraph
- Reading the concluding paragraph
- Deriving the main idea

Before students begin to read the text assignment, they should analyze the chapter title to discuss what might be included. Next, students skim through the chapter to locate and read any subtitles. The class should devise a question to be answered by reading that subsection. Students interpret graphs, maps, and charts for the gist of the information they summarize. Pictures are discussed to determine what they represent.

Next, students are asked to silently read the introductory and concluding paragraphs of the chapter. These paragraphs usually provide readers with some general ideas about the chapter. A brief discussion following their reading is recommended. In addition, students might examine the postreading questions provided at the chapter's end. Students should have a good idea of the chapter's contents by this time, so the Survey Technique is ended by having the students list ideas to be discussed in the chapter. From this, a main statement is developed about the overall theme of the chapter. At this point, students are prepared to enter the text more thoroughly.

Aukerman stated that this prereading strategy would take thirty minutes of instructional time in the classroom. During this time, teachers should demonstrate the strategy by explaining how to analyze the various parts of the text. The authors recommend that a time limit be imposed once students are familiar with the procedure. This necessitates skimming for information. Students then can independently survey the text chapter for information. A whole group discussion would follow to pool ideas derived by students, culminating with a purpose setting question. In this way, students get feedback on the ideas others are getting from the text and see how these ideas are organized into a main idea statement. Once students are able to verbalize what they are doing, they should not need teacher guidance, thus achieving the goal of active comprehension.

## Summary

This chapter provides a rationale for the use of questions in a prereading situation to stimulate curiosity, aid students in activating prior knowledge and anticipating information, and focus attention on important information. Strategies have been recommended which will allow teachers to provide guidance in the use of questioning and then to gradually withdraw their guidance until the expected learning outcome of using questions to set purposes for reading is achieved by the students. Active comprehension results, and students can use self-questioning to independently learn from text.

### References

Aukerman, R.C. *Reading in the secondary school.* New York: McGraw-Hill, 1972.

Betts, E.A. *Foundations of reading instruction.* New York: American Book, 1946.

Branley, F.M. (Ed.). *Reader's Digest science readers.* Pleasantville, NY: Reader's Digest Services, 1963.

Fillion, B. Reading as inquiry: An approach to literature learning. *English Journal,* 1981, *70,* 39-45.

Herber, H.L. *Teaching reading in content areas,* second edition. Englewood Cliffs, NJ: Prentice Hall, 1978.

Klauer, K.J. Intentional and incidental learning with instructional texts: A meta-analysis for 1970-1980. *American Educational Research Journal,* 1984, *21,* 323-339.

Manzo, A.V. The ReQuest procedure. *Journal of Reading,* 1969, *13,* 123-126.

Palincsar, A.S., and Brown, A.L. Reciprocal teaching of comprehension fostering and monitoring activities. *Cognition and Instruction,* 1984, *1,* 117-175.

Pearson, P.D., and Johnson, D.D. *Teaching reading comprehension.* New York: Holt, Rinehart & Winston, 1987.

Raphael, T.E. Teaching learners about sources of information for answering comprehension questions. *Journal of Reading,* 1984, *27,* 303-311.

Raphael, T.E. Teaching question answer relationships, revisited. *The Reading Teacher,* 1986, *39,* 516-522.

Readence, J.E., and Moore, D.W. Responding to literature: An alternative to questioning. *Journal of Reading,* 1979, *23,* 107-111.

Singer, H. Active comprehension: From answering to asking questions. *The Reading Teacher,* 1978, *31,* 901-908.

Singer, H., and Donlan, D. Active comprehension: Problem solving schema with question generation for comprehension of complex short stories. *Reading Research Quarterly,* 1982, *17,* 166-186.

Stauffer, R.G. *Directing reading maturity as a cognitive process.* New York: Harper & Row, 1969.

Thomas, K.J. The directed inquiry activity: An instructional procedure for content reading. In E.K. Dishner, T.W. Bean., J.E. Readence, and D.W. Moore (Eds.), *Reading in the content areas: Improving classroom instruction,* second edition. Dubuque, IA: Kendall/Hunt, 1986, 278-281.

Tierney, R.J., Readence, J.E., and Dishner, E.K. *Reading strategies and practices: A compendium,* second edition. Boston: Allyn & Bacon, 1985.

Wixson, K.K. Questions about a text: What you ask is what children learn. *The Reading Teacher,* 1983, *37,* 287-293.

Wong, B.Y.L. Self-questioning instructional research: A review. *Review of Educational Research,* 1985, *55,* 227-268.

# Chapter 3

# Forecasting Passages

| | |
|---|---|
| **Purpose** | *This chapter demonstrates the use of prediction as a means of motivating students, activating prior knowledge, and highlighting important concepts.* |

**Strategies**

1. The *Anticipation Guide* is designed to enhance comprehension by encouraging students to elaborate concepts in the text about which they may have prior knowledge.
2. The *PreReading Plan* provides students the opportunity to brainstorm about ideas to be presented in the text; to develop associations related to these ideas; and to elaborate, reflect, and rethink these ideas.
3. The *Visual Reading Guide* introduces students to a passage by examining the charts, graphs, diagrams, maps, and illustrations to formulate predictions about information in a text.

---

**R**eaders must rely on forecasting (predicting) to make sense of the passage to be read. Prediction is an essential process in the psycholinguistic and interactive models of reading (e.g., Goodman, 1985). Before reading, students must have some idea of what to expect in order to compare their expectations to what is being processed during reading. If the information being read is expected, the reading process is fluid, with optimal comprehension. If the information read is not expected, some decisions must be made.

Before reading the chapter, students formulate some hypotheses about what they expect to be reading. They may expect the text to give a general description of the solar system, discuss the sun, and then present information about individual planets, including temperature characteristics, makeup of the atmosphere, and number and size of satellites. As long as this is generally what students see, there is no problem. They probably will read some information they already know, plus some new information they may or may not find interesting and important.

But what happens if students read a sentence that states that the Earth's moon is made of green cheese? Based on the predictions (forecasts) the students have made, this information was not expected in a scientific discussion of the planets. Students have several options. One is to form an alternative plan to accept the information as fact and change their understanding of the moon; another is to trust initial impressions and try to combine prior knowledge with new information in a way that makes sense. Finally, students can assume that either they misread the passage or the author made an error. By rereading the statement, students finally see that the statement was read out of context and the author was stating that, in the past, people had *believed* the moon to be made of green cheese.

Forecasting a passage necessitates some uncertainty. Students cannot be sure that the information presented in the passage either will meet their expectations or will be wrong. Students also may discover that, while the author's information was correct, it was not presented in the expected format. Then, students must have enough flexibility to modify their expectations in order to understand the information presented in the passage.

Students who had not formed predictions about the information to be read probably would not have noticed any inconsistency in the passage. Unfortunately, many students read this way. They may have the prior knowledge necessary to understand the passage but the information is useless unless it is activated before reading. Students who do not forecast a passage have no expectations. When inconsistent information is presented, reading continues. No internal flag is raised to inform students that something is not making sense. Students then have trouble figuring out why the teacher will not accept their explanation about the makeup of the moon.

Finally, students can take the safe route and not read. Unfortunately, this path also is used by many students. Forecasting demands risk taking and some students are afraid to risk being wrong. While this attitude is safe, it defeats the purposes of education.

## Anticipation Guide

The Anticipation Guide is designed to enhance comprehension by encouraging students to focus attention on concepts to be covered in the text. Curiosity is aroused by challenging students' prior knowledge. Shablak and Castallo (1977) emphasize the key role played by conceptual conflict in stimulating curiosity by confronting students' prior knowledge. The use of controversy in motivating students to read in the content areas also has been discussed by Lunstrum (1981). Misconceptions students might have related to the content become the center for discussion and debate, forcing students to justify, modify, or delete prior knowledge. Prior knowledge then becomes the focus for predictions that will guide students through the passage.

The Anticipation Guide can be used with students at all levels with a variety of print and nonprint media. The chosen topic should be one about which students already have prior knowledge; totally unfamiliar topics are difficult to discuss. An Anticipation Guide is designed to prepare students to focus on specific concepts by creating a mismatch between their prior knowledge and the information to be learned. The overall purpose for reading becomes an attempt to resolve these differences.

The following steps can be used in the construction and implementation of an Anticipation Guide (Head & Readence, 1986). Each step is illustrated with an example pertaining to ecology.

1. *Identify the major concepts to be learned.* The content of the passage should be analyzed to decide the major points to be emphasized. Teachers do not want students to memorize every fact in a text; teachers want students to be able to identify and understand the major ideas. In a passage on the environment, the text focused on different types of pollution and on the potential limitations of our natural resources. The following concepts were identified as the most important for students to understand after the unit was completed.
   - There are limitations to the quantity and quality of our natural resources.
   - Alternate forms of energy need to be developed.
   - Our lives are being violated by many types of pollution involving land, water, air, and noise.
   - People are responsible for their environment.
2. *Determine whether the main concepts will support or challenge students' beliefs.* The teacher must decide what kinds of experiential backgrounds students possess related to the topic. (This process is discussed in Chapter 1.) Parents' attitudes, community values, and socioeconomic factors should be considered. Students whose parents are employed by a nuclear power plant might feel quite different about nuclear energy from students whose parents are antinuclear activists. It is important for teachers to respect individual students and not try to influence them to align with teachers' opinions. Students generally are reticent about volunteering opinions once teachers have expressed their feelings.
3. *Create three to five statements to support or challenge students' opinions.* The number of statements will vary depending on the age of the students,

level of topic familiarity, and number of major concepts. However, since each statement will be closely examined and discussed, five statements are plenty.

This step is one of the most crucial and is more difficult than it may seem initially. Good statements are most effective when students' prior knowledge about the topic is influenced by opinion rather than fact. When students are familiar with the topic, discussion is less effective. A common error in constructing Anticipation Guide statements is to use a factual sentence. A statement such as "The Environmental Protection Agency is housed in the Department of Agriculture" is dry, boring, and difficult to discuss. Students either know that it is correct or incorrect or they have no idea of the answer.

The following Anticipation Guide was constructed based on the major concepts identified in Step 1.

Directions: Before reading the following passage about ecology and the environment, read each of the following statements carefully. Put a check next to each one with which you agree. Be ready to discuss your decisions.

_____ a. There is little we can do to save our environment.

_____ b. Advancing technology is more important than protecting the environment.

_____ c. Nuclear power is the answer to our energy needs.

_____ d. Air pollution affects us all.

4. *Arrange the statements in the order you find to be the most appropriate and decide upon a presentation method.* The order of the statements could parallel their presentation in the text, or they could be arranged to allow for optimal discussion, i.e., most important to least important. The Anticipation Guide can be presented effectively through the use of overhead transparencies, chalkboards, or photocopies. Spaces for students to mark responses and directions appropriate for the level of the students should be included.

5. *Present the guide to the students.* Directions and statements should be read to the students before they work independently. Teachers should stress that students must be ready to defend their opinions during followup discussions. There are alternate methods for presenting the Anticipation Guide. One method is to have two columns before each statement, the first labeled *Me* and the second, *Author.* Students fill in the first column. While reading the text, students try to take on the role of the author, filling in the statements as they believe the author would. This format is illustrated here.

*Me*    *Author*

_____   _____   There is little we can do to save our environment.

_____   _____   Advancing technology is more important than protecting the environment.

_____   _____ Nuclear power is the answer to our energy needs.
_____   _____ Air pollution affects us all.

Another method is to label the first column *Anticipation* and the second *Reaction.* Before reading, students write their responses in the *Anticipation* column. After reading, students respond in the *Reaction* column. A combination of these two modifications is possible, using three columns labeled *Anticipation, Author,* and *Reaction.* Students respond before reading, read critically to determine the author's point of view, and then react after reading.

6. *Discuss each statement.* Discussion can take many forms. A good way to begin is to ask students to raise their hands if they agree/disagree with the statement. Volunteers from each group try to convince members of the opposing group to switch sides. Even quiet students can compare their thoughts with those of others in both groups, and can mentally evaluate their own statements. Discussion continues until each viewpoint has been considered and evaluated by the class. Another vote can be taken to see if anyone changed opinions.

A method more suitable for older students is to form discussion groups of four to six students. The members of the group must reach a consensus on each statement; if they cannot, they must explain why. After the groups have finished, a whole class discussion follows. This discussion can focus on getting the class to reach a consensus based on discussion from within the groups. It is important to note that agreement is not necessary, but students must try to analyze why they cannot reach agreement.

7. *Direct students to read the text.* The purpose for reading the text is now built-in. Students will read to find out if the information to be learned agrees with their thoughts and also to find additional information that will allow them to support, deny, or modify their original thoughts.

8. *Follow up discussion.* After reading, the class may get together to respond to the same statements using additional information gleaned from the text. If the me/author format was used, the discussion can be focused on similarities and differences between student and author responses, answering questions such as, "On which statements did you agree? Disagree? Why do you think the author does not agree with you? Did you change your mind as you read the passage? Do you *still* disagree with the author? Why? What could the author have done to convince you to change your opinion? What could you tell the author to try to change his/her opinion?" If the anticipation/ reaction format was used, similarities and differences between the two columns could be explored and discussed. The students should explain exactly what made them change their minds, and be ready to defend their new opinions.

The Anticipation Guide can be diagnostic in scope, assessing the prior knowledge of individual students. During the class discussion, individuals may be identified who would profit from alternative prereading or enrichment activities that expand on the subject to ensure an awareness of major concepts. Possible groupings of individuals may become apparent before valuable instructional time is used. Students who already display a firm grasp of the textual knowledge may be shifted to alternative areas of study.

Since the Anticipation Guide is teacher directed and based on information about which students have little prior knowledge, this strategy does not always lend itself to fading as well as some of the other strategies mentioned. However, the notion of having students ask themselves questions about the topic before they read (as discussed in Chapter 2) can be practiced through the use of the Anticipation Guide. After demonstrating the Guide's construct, the teacher could ask students with prior knowledge of the topic to help in the construction of the guide, thus leading students to independent construction of guides. Through group consensus, the best statements could be prepared for the rest of the class. In this way, some students could use their expertise to help others lacking mastery of the topic. Students might also lend a unique interpretation to the topic — one not previously considered by the teacher.

## PreReading Plan

The PreReading Plan (PREP) was developed by Langer (1981) as a method of using and analyzing students' prior knowledge. Teachers can use the information gained from the prereading lesson to tailor instruction to meet the needs of students at all grade levels. PREP can be used to prepare students to read, to view a movie or filmstrip, observe a classroom demonstration, or prepare for a field trip.

There are two major phases to implementing PREP in the classroom (Tierney, Readence, & Dishner, 1985). The first phase involves engaging students in a discussion of the key concepts relating to the topic. Teachers must decide on which concepts and on ways to elicit student discussion based on those concepts. (Chapter 1 details how teachers may develop expected learning outcomes.)

The discussion occurs in three steps.

1. *Initial associations with the concept.* At this step, teachers encourage students to elaborate about their prior knowledge on the topic. For instance, a teacher presenting a lesson on space exploration might ask, "What kinds of things come to mind when you think about the exploration of outer space? What would it be like to be an astronaut landing on an uncharted planet? What would you expect to see? Hear? Feel? Smell? Would you be afraid or anxious?" As students generate responses, the teacher writes them on the chalkboard. These questions should be divergent enough to allow students to recall a variety of prior information related to the topic.
2. *Reflecting on initial associations.* During this part of the discussion, stu-

dents reflect and elaborate on the ideas generated in Step 1. They should explain their responses. A teacher may ask, "Why would it be scary to be on an uncharted planet? Why do you think it would be quiet? Why do you think the planet would have no inhabitants? What things would make you afraid?" During this part of the discussion students clarify their ideas related to the topic. Students should be aware that there may not be agreement among all class members, but that is not a problem since each person will have his or her own associations.

3. *Reformulate knowledge.* During this phase of the discussion, the teacher asks students if they have new insights into the topic based on discussion in Steps 1 and 2, or if they wish to change any of the ideas previously presented. After the discussion in Step 3, students often come up with new associations not considered initially. Students are allowed to add, delete, or modify ideas.

In the second phase of PREP, the teacher analyzes the responses of individual students to assess the extent of individual knowledge related to the topic to be studied. Any misinformation a student may have that might cause problems with a lesson are noted. For instance, Julie's comment about going to Jupiter for a weekend vacation may indicate that she does not understand the length of time needed to travel through space, or her comment may be creative wishing.

During this analysis phase, the teacher can plan the best ways to teach the material to students. If many students have prior knowledge related to the topic to be studied, the teacher may want to include additional enrichment activities, or perhaps abbreviate sections of the chapter. The opposite may also happen. If the teacher feels that most of the students are not ready to begin this unit, some background teaching may be necessary to assure optimal learning.

While PREP (like the Anticipation Guide) is mainly teacher directed, the concepts behind PREP can be more easily transferred to student control. Through brainstorming prior knowledge, reflecting on the ideas, and reformulating thoughts, students can use the three discussion steps to question themselves before reading information from text. The teacher could informally critique students at each step, challenging them to preview lessons by relating prior knowledge to the topic of study. Students could be encouraged to independently apply PREP to difficult lessons in content areas. The teacher should emphasize the value of taking time for this prereading activity. A common complaint among students is, "You mean I *still* have to read it after all that?" If through teacher modeling, demonstration, and guided practice students can see the value in such an exercise, they are more likely to use this strategy.

## Visual Reading Guide

The Visual Reading Guide (Stein, 1978) is an approach for introducing students to a passage by predicting information based on graphics contained in the text. Reinking (1986) points out the need for instructional activities that help students draw connections between information presented in graphic aids, the text, and prior knowledge. Many times students ignore charts, maps, diagrams, and photographs, even though they offer important information that leads to understanding. Students seem to think that, because these visuals are not covered on a test, and are seldom discussed in class, they can be skipped. Students welcome photographs because they take up space and make chapters shorter.

Using the VRG, the teacher assesses expected learning outcomes, deciding which visuals support the information presented in the text and which maps or charts present information relating to the major concepts to be presented. Some graphics are not used in the VRG because they do not relate information essential to understanding the text. They may be helpful, but not really necessary to understanding main ideas presented in text. While reading, students are bombarded with information, so the teacher's job is to realistically limit the amount of information for which students will be held accountable. Presenting the VRG to students involves the following steps.

1. *Identification.* The teacher must explain to students why some graphics are more important than others. What are the qualities that make one chart important and another optional? When students are reading independently, this skill is crucial.

2. *Analysis.* Students should ascertain what each graphic is depicting. Some may have titles or headings, but these are not always accurate. Students should try to answer questions such as, "What is this showing me? How is this graphic organized? Why is this important to the topic we will be studying? Is there anything here that does not make sense? Why?"

3. *Discussion.* After the graphic has been analyzed for content, students should try to use the information to formulate a main idea, citing supporting evidence for their statement. As in the Anticipation Guide, students should try to reach a group consensus concerning information portrayed in the visual. To increase student involvement, the teacher may display the visual without its heading and ask students to supply information based on their prior knowledge.

Each visual is identified, analyzed, and discussed using the steps outlined. With teacher aid, students should be able to learn what to expect in a passage and to learn its important concepts. They will understand the teacher's expected learning outcomes and the content knowledge needed to understand the graphic.

Unlike the other strategies mentioned in this chapter, the VRG lends itself to fading. The teacher could model the strategy by explaining why some graphics are more important than others. This gives students an insight into the types of information the teacher finds important in the text. Through class discussions and guided practice, students gain insights into how the teacher and other students analyze visuals. This is particularly useful for those who may have problems understanding charts, maps, and diagrams. As slower students listen to the explanations of others, they gain their own insights into the information and they learn the thinking processes of more able students.

The teacher can aid the transfer of responsiblity to students by gradually turning over more of the class discussion to them. At first, the teacher may want to identify the important graphics, explain why each is important, discuss what the visuals show, and explain their importance to the topic (modeling). After students become familiar with this routine, the teacher limits his/her participation by identifying only the important graphics and allows the students to analyze and discuss each (guided practice). The end result is to have students independently identify, analyze, and explain the graphics important in understanding the topic being studied. This skill is especially useful for high school and college students who are responsible for large amounts of reading. The VRG may allow these students to focus on information related to the main ideas in the text. The goal is to create readers who can function independently of the teacher in the world outside of school.

## Summary

This chapter presents a rationale for the importance of activating prior knowledge before reading in order to predict meaning. Forecasting information in a passage allows the reader to form expectations which will guide the reading to follow. If the information being presented is consistent with expectations, the reading process is fluid; if the information is not consistent, the good reader learns to take steps to correct the inconsistencies. Three strategies that allow students to activate prior knowledge in order to forecast a passage have been presented. These strategies conform to the five factors that affect learning from text, presented in Chapter 1: expected learning outcomes, motivation, content knowledge, attention, and learning strategies. Suggestions were outlined for transferring these skills to promote independent learning.

### References

Goodman, K.S. Unity in reading. In H.Singer and R.B. Ruddell (Eds.), *Theoretical models and processes of reading,* third edition. Newark, DE: International Reading Association, 1985, 813-840.

Head, M.H., and Readence, J.E. Anticipation guides: Enhancing meaning through prediction. In E.K. Dishner, T.W. Bean. J.E. Readence, and D.W. Moore (Eds.), *Reading in the content areas: Improving classroom instruction,* second edition. Dubuque, IA: Kendall/Hunt, 1986, 229-234.

Langer, J.A. From theory to practice: A prereading plan. *Journal of Reading,* 1981, *25,* 152-156.

Lunstrum, J.P. Building motivation through the use of controversy. *Journal of Reading,* 1981, *24,* 687-691.

Reinking, D. Integrating graphic aids into content area instruction: The graphic information lesson. *Journal of Reading,* 1986, *30,* 146-151.

Shablak, S., and Castallo, R. Curiosity arousal and motivation in the teaching/learning
process. In H.L. Herber and R.T. Vacca (Eds.), *Research in reading in the content
areas: The third report.* Syracuse, NY: Syracuse University Reading and Language
Arts Center, 1977, 51-65.

Stein, H. The visual reading guide (VRG). *Social Education,* 1978, *42,* 534-535.

Tierney, R.J., Readence, J.E., and Dishner, E.K. *Reading strategies and practices: A
compendium,* second edition. Boston: Allyn & Bacon, 1985.

Chapter 4

# Understanding Vocabulary

<table>
<tr>
<td>Purpose</td>
<td>This chapter demonstrates the necessity of understanding new vocabulary in text to enhance students' comprehension and describes teaching and learning strategies that capitalize on context and categorization as ways to determine the meanings of new vocabulary.</td>
</tr>
</table>

Strategies

1. *Contextual Redefinition* helps students use context to make informed guesses about word meanings.
2. *Possible Sentences* aids students in predicting the meanings of unknown words and verifying their accuracy.
3. *List-Group-Label* activates students' prior knowledge about related concepts to be encountered in text.
4. *Feature Analysis* uses categorization as a systematic means of introducing and reinforcing word meanings.

Vocabulary knowledge plays a central role in reading comprehension. Not only does common sense tell us this, but research by Davis (1968) points out that students' comprehension of words predicts their comprehension of passages. There are many distinct views on why vocabulary knowledge is a major factor in passage comprehension. The number of word meanings readers know directly relates to their ability to comprehend text (Anderson & Freebody, 1981).

A search of the professional literature provides various recommendations for increasing students' vocabulary. Many strategies are available to acquaint students with new vocabulary such as vocabulary notebooks, increased free reading time, and discussing new terms as they are encountered. In many cases, these strategies entail developing content knowledge prior to reading. The strategies also provide the structure for teachers to fade their guidance so students can use them independently.

## Why Introduce New Vocabulary?

Readence, Bean, and Baldwin (1985) state that the role of content teachers should be to help students become *insiders* in their interaction with textbooks and subject matter. The following paragraph illustrates this point.

> Sometimes a mob might "grift" all day without "turning them over," but this is unlikely except in the case of a "jug mob" which takes a limited number of "pokes." Any pickpocket who has on his person more than one wallet is something of a hazard both to himself and to the mob, for each wallet can count as a separate offense if he should be caught. Therefore, it is safer to have cash only. "Class mobs" usually count the money each time they "skin the pokes," one stall commonly is responsible for all of it, and an accounting in full is made at the end of the day. When there is a woman with the mob, she usually carries the "knock up" (Maurer, 1955, p. 194).

Were you able to deal effectively with the terminology of the passage, or did you feel like an outsider due to your lack of awareness about pickpockets? Outsiders are restricted in their communication with a group because they cannot use the group's special vocabulary and the concepts inherent in that terminology. Insiders use special vocabulary freely to communicate with the collective members of a group. The analogy here is that students may be outsiders in the fields of science, social studies, or mathematics. They need to become insiders with the concepts of these subjects, and, to a large extent, this can be accomplished by introducing students to the technical vocabulary of these subjects.

Another argument for introducing the vocabulary of a content area is that "knowing" a word is not an all or nothing proposition. Using the term *gold* as an example, Anderson and Freebody (1981) point out that individuals probably would feel confident of its meaning and would know how to use the word in ordinary conversation. However, as in the pickpocket example, one would not feel so confident about knowing the meaning of gold when in the company of an ingroup such as jewelers or metallurgists. Additionally, you probably think of gold as a yellowish colored precious metal, but this is not necessarily true. First, not all gold is a yellowish color; and second, if a mountain of gold were discovered, it no longer would be considered precious. Thus, a word is defined by its context.

This notion ties directly into how a word will be defined in this chapter. A word is a pattern of auditory or visual symbols that represent schemata (Readence, Bean, & Baldwin, 1985). Such a definition implies that word meanings are in an endless stage of flux as the concepts words represent are being constantly modified by daily experiences. Content teachers should introduce the essential vocabulary students need to activate the appropriate schemata and enhance their comprehension of the text.

## Acquiring New Vocabulary

Vocabulary knowledge may be acquired through direct or indirect experiences. Direct experience occurs when students personally interact with what they are to learn. For instance, science class students may learn the concept of *refraction* by conducting an experiment with light and glass. This is the best way of learning new words, beginning at an early age. Vocabulary also may be acquired through indirect experiences, including films, television, pictures, and other media.

However, there are some concepts that cannot be learned either by direct or indirect experience. These are words which must be learned by making connections to known words. For instance, the concepts of *communism* or *depression* must be learned symbolically through association with other known vocabulary concepts. Not surprisingly, many of the words to be learned in content texts have to be learned symbolically. The prereading activities described in this chapter will help students learn new vocabulary symbolically by associating them with known vocabulary in context or through categorization.

Specific suggestions for teaching concepts through direct and indirect experiences will not be made in this volume; such an undertaking belongs in a discussion of specific content areas. Methods texts in social studies, physical and biological sciences, vocational arts, mathematics, and English suggest numerous direct and indirect experiences students can have with the particulars of their discipline.

## Principles of Vocabulary Instruction

Students do not automatically acquire new concepts and the ability to identify words that represent new concepts on their own. Direct instruction is essential, and almost any kind of instruction is better than none at all. Graves (1986) found that providing the meanings of words, practicing their meanings, and learning meanings from context were better than no instruction at all for average and below average middle school readers. Therefore, one principle of effective vocabulary instruction is to provide students with instruction for potentially troublesome words.

Johnson and Pearson (1984) point out two important principles of effective vocabulary instruction. First, the importance of practice with new words cannot be underestimated. Students should be given an opportunity to use new vocabulary to reinforce their grasp of word meanings. Second, there is no substitute for the enthusiasm teachers can convey about the value of acquiring new vocabulary.

Teachers can be effective models by using the words students are expected to learn.

A final principle of effective vocabulary instruction is eclecticism in teaching. Students learn in a variety of ways; therefore, successful vocabulary instruction calls for a repertoire of activities. Prereading activities for helping students assimilate new vocabulary are divided between those that focus on helping students infer the meanings of words by the way they are used in a passage, and those that emphasize categorization of words.

Context and categorization are not the only methods of emphasizing vocabulary prior to assigning a reading passage. They do, however, complement the ones suggested in earlier chapters of this monograph. (For a more complete view of methods for teaching meaning vocabulary, see Dale, O'Rourke, & Bamman, 1971 and Graves, 1986.)

## Inferring Word Meanings from Context

This section describes two teaching strategies—Contextual Redefinition and Possible Sentences. These strategies emphasize context as an avenue to vocabulary development.

## Contextual Redefinition

All human experience is dependent upon context, a necessary and natural part of reading and comprehending. Many reading educators stress the importance of using context in verifying and interpreting the meanings of words which, in turn, leads to more effective processing of print. The use of context also allows readers to make informed guesses about the meaning of words in print and to monitor those guesses by checking them for accuracy as reading continues. In essence, context enables readers to predict a word's meaning by making connections between their prior knowledge and the text.

Frequently, writers provide various direct clues to the meanings of words in sentences. These clues might include the use of synonyms, a description or definition, familiar expressons, or comparison and contrast with other concepts. While it might not be important for students to identify which type of context clue is provided, it is essential that they be able to use these devices to derive meaning. The following teaching strategy, Contextual Redefinition (Cunningham, Cunningham, & Arthur, 1981; Readence, Bean, & Baldwin, 1985), provides a format for students to realize the importance of context in ascertaining meaning.

To demonstrate the strategy, consider the words *vapid, lummox,* and *piebald.* Would you be able to provide a definition for these terms? If not, read the following sentences to see if they help.

1. Even though she intended to discuss a lively issue, her conversation with me was *vapid,* lacking animation and force.

2. As a result of his ungainly, slovenly appearance, Bill was often unjustly labeled a *lummox.*
3. Though described as *piebald* because of its spotted black and white colors, the horse was still considered beautiful by many horse lovers.

If you did not already know the meanings of the terms, the sentences probably were helpful in determining the meanings. Good readers use context, often subconsciously, as a clue to meaning. Many students who are not efficient readers do not effectively use context, particularly when they face new information in subject matter textbooks. Teachers can greatly enhance students' ability to comprehend text by teaching them the use of context, instead of assuming they already use the strategy.

Contextual Redefinition entails the following steps.

1. *Select unfamiliar words.* Identify words students will encounter in text that are central to comprehending important concepts and may present trouble for students as they read.
2. *Write a sentence.* Provide a context for each word with appropriate clues to the word's meaning. If such a context already exists, use it. In the examples presented with *vapid, lummox,* and *piebald,* clues of definition or description were provided.
3. *Present the words in isolation.* Using a transparency or chalkboard, ask students to provide a meaning for each word. Students defend their guesses and, as a group, come to some consensus as to the best definition. An accurate meaning may be offered, but many times the guesses might be humorous or even off the wall; this is part of the process of realizing the importance of context in vocabulary learning.
4. *Present the words in a sentence.* Using the sentence or short paragraph previously developed, present the word in its appropriate context. Again, students should be asked to offer guesses as to the meaning of each word and to defend their definitions. In this way less able readers will be able to experience the thinking processes involved in deriving a definition from context. In essence, students act as models of appropriate reading behavior for one another.
5. *Dictionary verification.* Students then consult a dictionary to verify the meaning.

It is important for teachers to model their thinking in using context and to demonstrate the use of Contextual Redefinition before expecting students to use the strategy.

It is imperative for teachers to remember that Contextual Redefinition is a strategy that only introduces new vocabulary words. After reading and discussing the words in class, teachers need to provide students postreading situations to broaden and reinforce their understanding of the words. Additional practice gives students more of an opportunity to retain newly learned words in long term memory for later use.

Several benefits can be derived from the use of Contextual Redefinition. Students should realize that (1) simply guessing the meaning of a word in isolation is frustrating, haphazard, and probably not very accurate; (2) context provides clues to the meaning of words which allows informed guesses that may approximate dictionary definitions; and (3) motivation is necessary to discover the meaning of unknown words rather than to passively remember vocabulary terms. Students have the potential to independently apply informed guessing through context in other forms of reading.

## Possible Sentences

Possible Sentences (Moore & Moore, 1986) is a combination vocabulary/prediction activity designed to acquaint students with new vocabulary in their reading, guide them in verifying the accuracy of the statements they generate, and arouse curiosity concerning the passage to be read. Possible Sentences is best used when unfamiliar vocabulary is mixed with familiar terminology.

Possible Sentences consists of five steps.

1. List key vocabulary
2. Elicit sentences
3. Read in order to verify sentences
4. Evaluate sentences
5. Generate new sentences

The following example text will be used to describe Possible Sentences. The length of this text is not typical of students' reading assignments but does serve to illustrate the strategy being discussed.

### Warts Still Defy Spunk Water and More Scientific Cures

Utter medical humility certainly was displayed by dermatologists at the University of Cincinnati when they announced that after a 20 year study of warts, they were no nearer finding a satisfactory cure than when they started. Although the scientists concluded that the verrucae are produced by a polyoma virus, a highly contagious carrier, they confessed that they weren't really further advanced than Hippocrates in suggesting reasons for the incidence of warts, or nostrums for their cure. This leaves orthodox doctors with treatments such as caustic painting, freezing, or electrocautery.

Warts tend to come and go at their own volition. Their evanescence has made them a target for old wives' charms and autosuggestive cures. And such folk medicine doesn't seem to have progressed any better down the decades than that of professional practitioners. Pliny the Elder, in the First Century A.D., advised afflicted Romans to touch each of their nodules with a pea, wrap the peas in a cloth, and throw the parcel away behind them. The magical theory was the symbolic transference of evil in which the person picking up the package would pick up warts as well.

The popularity of Tom Sawyer has led to widespread reliance among rural and verrucose Americans on Tom Sawyer's prescription of sprinkling with "spunk water," rainwater scooped up from a tree stump in the woods. Interestingly, spunk water never existed in the American language until Mark Twain dreamed it up (adapted from Ryan, 1977).

To determine the key vocabulary, the following concepts are selected as most important.

- Medical science has not been able to find a cure for warts.
- Current treatments consist of caustic painting, freezing, and electrocautery.
- Folk cures for warts have descended through the ages.

1. *List key vocabulary.* In order to lead students to the above concepts, list the following vocabulary on the chalkboard and pronounce each word as you write it.

*Warts*

| | |
|---|---|
| dermatologists | electrocautery |
| verrucae | autosuggestive cures |
| polyoma virus | Pliny the Elder |
| nostrums | verrucose |
| caustic painting | spunk water |
| freezing | Mark Twain |

2. *Elicit sentences.* Ask students to select at least two words from the list and formulate a sentence using the words. The resulting sentence must be one they think might be in the text. It is useful for the teacher to model a possible sentence and the thinking required in formulating one. Record the sentences verbatim, even if the information is not correct, and underline the words used from the list. Students may use words already in sentences provided that a new context is created. Cease recording the sentences after a specified period of time, when all the words have been used, or when the students can produce no more. Below are some sentences that might be elicited using Possible Sentences.

   (a) Freezing and electrocautery are two methods dermatologists use to remove warts.
   (b) Three types of warts are verrucae, nostrums, and verrucose.
   (c) Mark Twain said to use spunk water for removing warts.
   (d) Three home remedies for removing warts are spunk water, autosuggestive cures, and caustic painting.
   (e) Pliny the Elder discovered the polyoma virus.

3. *Read to verify sentences.* Have students read the text selection for the explicit purpose of verifying the accuracy of their possible sentences.

4. *Evaluate sentences.* After the reading, have students evaluate each sentence. The text selection may be used as a reference. Evaluate sentences according

to their accuracy, and refine or omit those that are inaccurate. Such discussion calls for careful reading, and judgments of the accuracy of the generated sentences must be defended. Thus, students model their thinking for one another. Examining the possible sentences above, sentences (a) and (c) may be accepted as they stand. Sentence (b) will have to be modified because *verrucae* is the only word listed in the sentence that is synonymous with warts. This sentence might be modified to the following: *Verrucose* people are constantly seeking *nostrums* for the cure of their *verrucae*. Sentence (d) can be modified by dropping out *caustic painting* as a home cure since it is a remedy used by dermatologists. Finally, sentence (e) has to be modified since *Pliny the Elder* did not discover the *polyoma virus*. It could be modified as follows: *Pliny the Elder,* unaware that warts are caused by the *polyoma virus,* suggested a folk remedy for getting rid of warts.

5. *Generate new sentences.* After evaluation and modificaton of the original sentences are accomplished, ask students for new sentences. New sentences are generated with the intent of extending student understanding of the text concepts. As these sentences are dictated, have students check them for accuracy, using the text selection for confirmation. Students should record all final acceptable sentences in their notebooks.

Possible Sentences provides students an opportunity to practice their language skills. Using their prior knowledge, students think of and evaluate possible connections new vocabulary terms may have. They speak to express their associations and listen to others' thoughts and associations. They read to verify the possible combinations and discuss their findings in postreading situations. Finally, students use their newly gained content knowledge with their prior knowledge to practice other possible sentence combinations which will allow them to continue to extend and reinforce their meanings for the vocabulary terms.

## Fading Instruction with Context

The purpose of using context as a learning strategy is to get students to make tentative predictions about the meanings of words using their prior knowledge and, subsequently, to use context independently as a means to verify their guesses. Demonstration by the teacher and guided practice for the students help students understand the process of using context to infer meaning. Merely telling students that using context when they read text assignments will be helpful in inferring meanings of unfamiliar words may not be enough.

Teachers need to explain context and model its use. After one or two demonstration sessions, guided practice should be provided, with students using context repeatedly and with teacher feedback and reteaching when appropriate. Teachers provide sentences containing relevant unknown words and ask students to predict their meaning, using the context. Students explain to the class how they used the context to arrive at a word's meaning, compare their explanations about how they used context, and receive feedback concerning accuracy from the teacher and other students.

Opportunities need to be provided for students to learn to use context on their own. Students in small groups are more apt to actively participate in the learning situation. The whole class could be used as a forum with the teacher providing feedback to the small groups on the accuracy of their use of context and the thinking involved. It is important for the teacher to find out if students can verbalize how to use context. If they can, they probably can use context successfully on their own.

Fading can begin by having students work on their own before they meet in small groups. Differences in their predictions about meanings of words can be worked out in the small group before the teacher works with them in the large group. Next, students would work independently without the small group. Feedback would be given on their application of the strategy in the large group only. Finally, as a test of a true independent application of the strategy, feedback would not be given to the large group, and individual assistance would be provided only as needed. This emulates the type of situation students would be involved in if they were actually reading on their own. The only difference is that the teacher provided students the key words from the text; in true independent reading situations, students would have to decide the importance of words as they encounter them and use context to infer the meanings. The dictionary would remain the source for checking the accuracy of predicted word meanings.

## Categorizing Words

Whether using Possible Sentences, Contextual Redefinition, or other strategies designed to introduce vocabulary, context serves as the vehicle for verifying tentative guesses about the meanings of unknown words. However, while determining meaning, context may not always reveal it (Johnson & Pearson, 1984; Schatz & Baldwin, 1986). Teachers need to clarify the meanings of important vocabulary terms. While this may not seem desirable, we are not suggesting that telling students the meaning of unknown words means providing short definitions or synonyms for them. A study of words in this way is a very narrow approach to vocabulary development because it neglects important relationships that add depth to word meanings.

When we advise telling students the meanings of new vocabulary, we are advocating two systematic teaching strategies to develop concepts based on students' prior knowledge. Procedures to teach word concepts developed by Taba (1967) and Johnson and Pearson (1984) deserve consideration. The expected learning outcome resulting from these strategies is that students will be able to use categorization as a means to understand new vocabulary and accompanying concepts.

## List-Group-Label

The List-Group-Label lesson was originally conceived by Taba (1967) as a vocabulary development activity in social studies and science. It is based on the use of categorization as a way to teach students to organize their verbal concepts. Thus, List-Group-Label is most appropriate when many of the concepts are familiar so prior knowledge can be activated and connections made to the topic.

The lesson begins with the teacher supplying students with a stimulus topic drawn from their experiences or from the materials they are studying. Next, students develop a list of words they associate with the topic. A spiraling effect occurs; i.e., initial associations with the topic promote more associations and connections by other students. The teacher records the associations until the list totals twenty-five to thirty words. The students then construct smaller lists of words from the large list and provide a label for each grouping. Approximately three to five words are placed in the smaller groups, and students then explain why they have grouped words in a particular manner.

When used as a prereading strategy, the List-Group-Label lesson is designed to activate students' content knowledge, thereby enhancing comprehension. To exemplify its use as a prereading activity in the content areas, the stimulus topic *geometry* will be demonstrated as used in a seventh grade math class. The students were briefly introduced to geometry in sixth grade, but the seventh grade curriculum called for a lengthier study. To reinforce the unit, the teacher used the format of the List-Group-Label lesson. The students generated the following list of words.

*Geometry*

| | |
|---|---|
| square | rectangle |
| cubic centimeters | triangular prism |
| math | base |
| volume | side |
| area | cylinder |
| cube | prism |
| pyramid | face |
| cone | edge |
| sphere | corner |
| symmetry | congruence |
| ruler | surface |
| protractor | compass |
| square inches | circle |
| equilateral triangle | |

The students next made smaller groups of words from the list and labeled them. Following are examples of these groups.

- Protractor, ruler, compass = measurement tools.
- Sphere, cone, circle, cylinder = curved surfaces.
- Square inches, volume, area, cubic centimeters = forms of measurements.
- Cylinder, prism, cube, pyramid, square = things that have faces.
- Prism, cone, cube, triangular prism = space figures.
- Square, sphere, corner, volume, circle = words with six letters.
- Side, symmetry, square, square inches, surface = words beginning with *s*.

As can be seen, the majority of the groups are based on meaningful, semantic associations. However, the last two groups are based on surface level spelling cues rather than semantic cues. This is not the desired outcome of the List-Group-Label lesson even though such associations might serve as important mnemonic devices for some students as they deal with the text material. The purpose of this lesson is to stimulate meaningful word associations, thereby activating students' prior knowledge.

The List-Group-Label lesson also may be used as a follow up activity in the postreading stage of a content area lesson. The steps are identical, but the purpose is different. In the postreading stage, this strategy is used for review and reinforcement of text concepts; i.e., students are encouraged to use the content knowledge they have gained from the text in addition to related prior knowledge to form groups and label them. The List-Group-Label lesson also helps teachers ascertain whether students have learned the important text concepts.

## Feature Analysis

Feature Analysis is intended to provide students with a systematic teaching procedure for exploring, reinforcing, and organizing vocabulary concepts through categorization (Johnson & Pearson, 1984). This strategy is somewhat complex and should be used with relatively sophisticated students.

Feature Analysis is composed of the following steps.

1. *Category selection.* It is best to begin this strategy with a text topic familiar to the students. Once acquainted with Feature Analysis, categories may become less well known. Planets of the solar system will be the category used here.

2. *List category terms.* The teacher provides terms for concepts or objects connected to the category topic. These terms can be provided by students once they are accustomed to the strategy. In the case of our category, the following planet names might be introduced: Mercury, Venus, Earth, and Mars.

3. *List features.* The teacher or students must now decide which features to explore. It is best to start with a few features and add more later in the lesson. For instance, features to be examined are whether the planets are hot,

cold, big, small, and life supporting. After these steps have been completed, the following feature matrix should result.

*Planets*

|  | hot | cold | big | small | life |
|---|---|---|---|---|---|
| Mercury |  |  |  |  |  |
| Venus |  |  |  |  |  |
| Earth |  |  |  |  |  |
| Mars |  |  |  |  |  |

4. *Indicate feature possession.* Students are guided through the feature matrix for the purpose of deciding whether a particular planet possesses each of the features. Teachers should first demonstrate how to deal with the matrix by modeling their thinking. It is recommended that a simple plus/minus (+/–) system be used initially to indicate feature possession. Later, a more sophisticated system such as a Likert scale (1 = always, 2 = some, 3 = never) may be used when students become familiar with Feature Analysis and want to explore the relative degree of feature possession. Feature possession should be based on typical patterns; i.e., a plus sign indicates that a category item *usually* has the feature. The presence of similar signs in opposite features can indicate a third feature. For example, if a planet is neither big nor small, it is medium sized. Through demonstration and guided practice, the feature matrix for planets should look like the following, using a +/– system.

*Planets*

|  | hot | cold | big | small | life |
|---|---|---|---|---|---|
| Mercury | + | – | – | + | – |
| Venus | + | – | – | – | – |
| Earth | – | – | – | – | + |
| Mars | – | – | – | + | – |

5. *Add terms/features.* The matrix should be expanded by adding new terms to be explored—in this case, the rest of the planets—and new features to be analyzed—in this case, the presence of rings and moons. The students can generate these items in an attempt to further expand their knowledge concerning the topic. (This step can be eliminated once students are familiar with, and motivated to use, the strategy by using all terms and features in the initial matrix.)

6. *Complete and explore matrix.* The final step is to complete the expanded matrix and form generalizations about the category terms. The completed matrix should look like the following.

|  | hot | cold | big | small | life | rings | moons |
|---|---|---|---|---|---|---|---|
| Mercury | + | − | − | + | − | − | − |
| Venus | + | − | − | − | − | − | − |
| Earth | − | − | − | − | + | − | + |
| Mars | − | − | − | + | − | − | + |
| Jupiter | − | + | + | − | − | + | + |
| Saturn | − | + | + | − | − | + | + |
| Uranus | − | + | + | − | − | + | + |
| Neptune | − | + | + | − | − | − | + |
| Pluto | − | + | − | + | − | − | − |

*Planets*

Exploration of the matrix commences with its completion. This entails students examining how the terms (planets) are similar, yet unique. The teacher can demonstrate this by noting that while the Earth shares a number of characteristics with other planets, it is the only planet that is life supporting. Later, questions can be asked to motivate students' observations. Finally, have students make their own connections by noting similarities and differences. Some questions students could be asked are: Which planets are the coldest? Which have moons? How is Pluto different from Mars? What makes Earth a unique planet? Which planet is most like Earth? Why? As students interact, divergent comments and changes in the matrix are welcome as long as their reasoning is sound. When the exploration is completed, students should be directed to read the text to verify their categorizations.

Postreading activities with Feature Analysis revolve around a discussion of the accuracy of the categorization in prereading. Corrections are made if support from the text is cited. Additionally, students can further expand the matrix by adding text knowledge they have picked up while reading. The final corrected and expanded feature matrix is then copied into students' notebooks as additional reinforcement and a source for study.

## Fading Instruction with Categorization

The purpose of categorization is to help students develop their vocabulary by attending to relationships among words. The ultimate goal of categorization is to teach students to apply it independently in their reading assignments. However, since the categorization strategies are teacher directed and may be based on information for which students have little prior knowledge, categorization does not lend itself to fading as well as strategies which utilize context.

Nevertheless, teachers can progressively withdraw their involvement in these learning situations by using a technique of moving from a whole group to a small group to an individual format as students become accustomed to using categorization. Small groups can provide an effective format for students to collaboratively use categorization as a means of developing their content knowledge. Students who possess extensive prior knowledge of a particular topic may be able to independently brainstorm their own categories related to a topic under study in prereading. Then these students can be directed to read to verify their categories and expand them in postreading. For those students, categorization can serve as an independent study aid when the teacher is not available for feedback.

## Summary

This chapter has presented a rationale for introducing text vocabulary and principles essential to effective vocabulary development. Four teaching strategies have been presented to aid teachers in developing students' vocabularies. Contextual Redefinition can be used when a few words can be defined by the context in which they occur. Possible Sentences is appropriate when unfamiliar vocabulary is mixed with familiar terminology so students can attempt to associate new information with known information. When context doesn't work, two activities were advocated for teaching new vocabulary using concept development models—List-Group-Label and Feature Analysis.

The importance of such direct instruction in vocabulary development cannot be overemphasized. Additionally, using strategies which involve students in discovering the meaning of new words and provide a potential format for independent learning are essential.

### References

Anderson, R.C., and Freebody, P. Vocabulary knowledge. In J.T. Guthrie (Ed.), *Comprehension and teaching: Research reviews.* Newark, DE: International Reading Association, 1981, 77-117.

Cunningham, J.W., Cunningham, P.M., and Arthur, S.V. *Middle and secondary school reading.* New York: Longman, 1981.

Dale, E., O'Rourke, J., and Bamman, H.A. *Techniques of teaching vocabulary.* Palo Alto, CA: Field Educational Publications, 1971.

Davis, F.B. Research in comprehension in reading. *Reading Research Quarterly,* 1968, *3,* 499-545.

Graves, M.F. Vocabulary learning and instruction. In E.Z. Rothkopf (Ed.), *Review of research in education,* volume 13. Washington, DC: American Educational Research Association, 1986, 49-89.

Johnson, D.D., and Pearson, P.D. *Teaching reading vocabulary,* second edition. New York: Holt, Rinehart & Winston, 1984.

Maurer, D.W. *Whiz mob.* Schenectady, NY: New College and University Press, 1964.

Moore, D.W., and Moore, S.A. Possible sentences. In E.K. Dishner, T.W. Bean, J.E. Readence, and D.W. Moore (Eds.), *Reading in the content areas: Improving classroom instruction,* second edition. Dubuque, IA: Kendall/Hunt, 1986.

Readence, J.E., Bean, T.W., and Baldwin, R.S. *Content area reading: An integrated approach,* second edition. Dubuque, IA: Kendall/Hunt, 1985.

Ryan, P. Warts still defy spunk water and more scientific cures. *Smithsonian*, 1977, *7*, 164.

Schatz, E.K., and Baldwin, R.S. Context clues are unreliable predictors of word meaning. *Reading Research Quarterly*, 1986, *21*, 439-453.

Taba, H. *Teacher's handbook for elementary social studies*. Reading, MA: Addison-Wesley, 1967.

Chapter 5

# Graphically Representing Information

| **Purpose** | *This chapter demonstrates the effectiveness of previewing information to be learned in a passage using a graphic representation which allows students to see how concepts are related within the context of a chapter of text or unit of study.* |
|---|---|

**Strategies**
1. The *Web* allows students to note the relationships among concepts presented in the text.
2. The *Graphic Organizer* presents a schematic diagram of major concepts and additional terms which convey the text structure to students before reading.
3. The *Outline* organizes major concepts and pertinent details in a hierarchical organization.
4. The *Word Map* visually depicts the definition of a word and the concept it represents, including primary properties of the word and examples.

Graphic representations of information depict relationships among concepts so that students have a map of an upcoming passage or unit lesson. Just as maps are useful for travelers wishing to reach a desired location without getting lost, graphic representations of text can allow readers to navigate their way through what they read. Webbing, graphic organizers, and outlines depict the organization of textual material, enabling students to be guided through information that is important to learn and remember. The word map explores nuances of word meanings, delving much deeper than traditional vocabulary instruction and graphically analyzing the meanings. Graphically representing information through these techniques provides students with a framework for previewing and reading a passage. Students learn to anticipate expected learning outcomes, as outlined in Chapter 1. As discussed in Chapter 3, these expectations can form the basis for making judgments while reading that can directly enhance comprehension. In this way, information can be assimilated more readily than if students are thrust into a passage with no preparation other than "Read Chapter 9 for tomorrow. Be ready to discuss it."

The positive effects of graphically representing text can be explained by schema theory (Rumelhart & Ortony, 1977). A schema is a framework for how individuals view the world and is closely tied to prior knowledge. This framework forms the basis for integrating new information. Schemata also represent individual beliefs and perceptions. Since new information being processed must filter through these schemata in some way, being able to activate prior knowledge is essential before new information can be integrated into long term memory. The quality and quantity of new information learned, therefore, are closely related to the quality and quantity of what is already known; i.e., schemata/prior knowledge.

Research (Beck, Omanson, & McKeown, 1982; DiVesta, Schultz, & Dangel, 1973) has established that comprehension can be enhanced by identifying the instructional framework of a text and giving students the tools necessary for structuring that information. For example, expository text is structured in a factual, objective way. On the other hand, literary text usually engages students' interests by drawing them into a story. Students who can identify the differences between these structures can more easily form expectations on which to base their reading predictions. Graphic depictions of text structure enables students to become familiar with text structure while reading, allowing them to become independent readers, learners, and thinkers.

The following strategies (1) allow students to observe and learn methods for structuring new information so it can be more readily understood, and (2) give students experiences with text and the structure of textual concepts so they may individually acquire reading/thinking strategies.

## Web

The web is a method for visually graphing the structure of the text to define and show important relationships among major concepts to be presented. Webs can be constructed for different sections of a text, depending on how indepth the focus of the study will be. For instance, with younger students, a web can be constructed for a paragraph from a unit of study. In this case, almost all main ideas and details can be integrated into the web. This may work well for a paragraph that has a large number of important concepts traditionally difficult for students to comprehend. Older students may construct a web for an entire chapter of content text. In this case, many details will be omitted for the sake of convenience, and only ideas which directly support the main ideas will be included. This forces students to pay attention to details, including in the web only those essential to the overall understanding of the text. The center of the web contains the main idea(s), and the spokes radiating from the web contain related information. The shape of the web is determined by the text being studied. There is no standard format that all webs follow. Different types of text would dictate different types of structures. Reutzel (1985) outlined several examples for exposition, compare/contrast, and cause/effect. Clewell and Haldemos (1983) outlined several steps for constructing a web.

1. *Draw a circle for the center of the web.* This circle should be larger than all others and heavily outlined to show that it is the hub around which all the other ideas emanate.
2. *Write the main idea from the paragraph, page, or chapter in the center of the circle.* This should be one or two words which best summarize the main idea. This should also be written in bold letters to draw attention to it.
3. *List supporting information related to the main idea.* Students should brainstorm ideas for several minutes, listing words related to the key word or phrase. These ideas should be written on the chalkboard for future reference.
4. *Create the web by placing key words or phrases on new spokes until ideas are exhausted.* Information which is directly related to the main idea should be identified and listed in smaller circles at the end of spokes emanating from the center circle. Next, words or phrases which relate to the main ideas are identified from the brainstormed list. These words are written at the end of the spokes. It is important to note that word spokes also can emanate from details to which they are related. Thus, an idea may be two or more spokes away from the center of the web.
5. *The class explores and discusses the web, adding, deleting, or modifying ideas as needed.* During this step, students can compare their own prior knowledge to the structure of the web, become aware of new words, and relate new words and knowledge to those that are already known. Through class discussion, the teacher can assess an individual student's abilities in order to make instructional decisions.

A web for a chapter in social studies introducing the state of Pennsylvania might look like Figure 1.

Webs for fictional stories can be constructed from basal readers or from literature studies in language arts and English (Sinatra, Stahl-Gemake, & Berg, 1984). These webs would depict elements of the story and give students practice in identifying story structure. Webs can be effectively employed during prereading to focus students' attention on the main ideas, vocabulary, and structure of the text. Since brainstorming a story with which students are unfamiliar is difficult, the

Figure 1

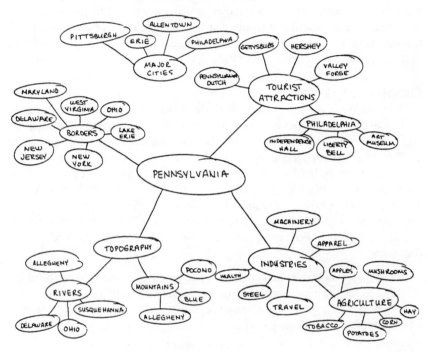

teacher could use the opportunity to provide the students with main idea and detail terms before reading. As students read or study the lesson, they try to create a web which places the terms in a structure that makes sense to them. These individual webs then could be used to promote postreading class discussions.

Webs can be used after reading to review the major ideas and their relationships presented in a lesson. The teacher provides the major topics and students fill in related details from the text during and after reading. In other related activity, the teacher provides a web form with several of the words filled in. From a list provided by the teacher, students fill in the remaining terms to construct a web that fits the ideas into a structure that makes sense.

The web can be used independently by students. The teacher can demonstrate how main ideas and details from text fit together. These can be discussed before a chapter is read, allowing students to use the teacher made web during reading to help connect information. Guided practice would involve students in completing web templates started by the teacher but with some information missing. As students read, they are charged with supplying the missing information. A follow up class discussion can weigh students' copies as good or poor choices, keeping in mind that webs need not be identical. A key to fading instruction is that students must be made aware of the advantages of using a web. Through demonstration and small group practice students can become more adept at this task. With teacher motivation students can use webs independently for study aids for tests and other classroom related activities.

## Graphic Organizer

The Graphic Organizer (Barron & Earle, 1973), also known as the structured overview, presents a schematic diagram for major concepts and additional terms which convey information to students before they read. This strategy has been used primarily with secondary students, but Boothby and Alvermann (1984) found that it can be used successfully with students in the fourth grade. It can be easily adapted to many content areas (Earle, 1976; Lunstrum & Taylor, 1978; Thelen, 1984). Tierney, Readence, and Dishner (1985) explain how a graphic organizer also can be used as a point of reference when students begin to read and study in detail. Following are steps used in the construction of a graphic organizer.

1. The major objectives and concepts to be taught are identified by the teacher. The following concepts and terms were identified from a chapter on "Fibers" in *Steps in Clothing Skill* (Draper & Bailey, 1978) which could be used in a secondary home economics class.

*Key Concepts*
- Fibers can be either natural or man made.
- Natural fibers can be obtained from animals or vegetables; man made fibers are chemically produced.
- Examples of natural fibers include cotton, linen, wool, and silk.
- Examples of man made fibers include acrylic, rayon, nylon, polyester, and acetate.

*Key Terms*

| fiber | acrylic | silkworm |
|-------|---------|----------|
| yarn | nylon | cocoon |
| fabric | acetate | man made fibers |
| cotton | linen | rayon |
| flax | wool | polyester |

2. The key terms are arranged into a diagram which parallels the text structure, stressing relationships between and among terms. Depicting text relationships may be considered to be one advantage of a graphic organizer over an outline. The structure can take many forms, although coordinate terms

should be at parallel levels. Notice that this is different from webs, where the terms surround the main ideas, and coordinate terms may be at different places around the wheel. Terms may be deleted or others added from the previous list in order to make the organizer more coherent. The teacher should consider the students' background of information and the organization of the text when constructing the organizer. One diagram that would be appropriate for this chapter is shown. Different diagrams could be drawn for the same passage to determine a "best fit" for different groups of students, based on ability and prior knowledge.

3. Present the graphic organizer to the class. A chalkboard can be used to present the organizer to the students, but an overhead projector is recommended. Smith (1979) advised that the diagram be presented to the students little by little. This can be accomplished by using a piece of paper on top of the transparency. The teacher talks the students through the diagram, explaining any unclear relationships and encouraging discussion of key points. Each section is presented and discussed until the entire diagram has been displayed. After discussion, the diagram can be left in place for use as a reference during silent reading and subsequent discussion.

The graphic organizer can be a powerful tool for helping students. If a reader wonders how the author jumped from topic *A* to topic *B,* a quick glance at the graphic organizer can resolve the uncertainties.

A graphic organizer often can be made to reflect the text structure of the author. van Dijk and Kintsch (1983) established the importance of a reader's knowledge of the structure of a text in making predictions for reading. A well organized text demands less of a student's attention while reading than a poorly structured text. Readence, Bean, and Baldwin (1985) illustrate different types of graphic organizers that relate to text structures.

A graphic organizer can be used by students when surveying a text (see Chapter 2). An incomplete diagram is displayed and students are told which text pat-

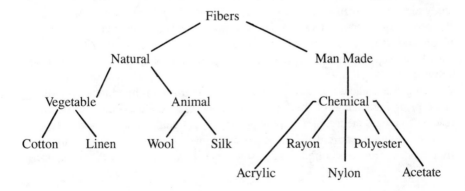

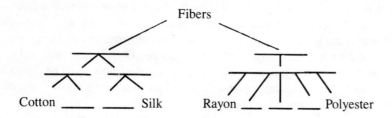

Fibers

Cotton ____ ____ Silk     Rayon ____ ____ ____ Polyester

tern of organization the author has used. The students survey the chapter in order to fill in the missing sections of the organizer.

As with webs, an incomplete diagram can be used after the students have read a passage using a postorganizer. Readence and Moore (1979) point out that the same diagram used to enhance readiness in the prereading stage can be used to aid in the recall of material after reading. For instance, blanks can be left in the original diagram for students to fill in by recalling the organization of the new text material learned during silent reading. Deleted words are listed in random order underneath the diagram. A graphic postorganizer for our "Fibers" chapter might look like this.

| | |
|---|---|
| Vegetable | Animal |
| Acetate | Nylon |
| Wool | Linen |
| Man made | Acrylic |

Students either recall or locate appropriate terms and concepts in order to complete the diagram. This form can be put on a ditto sheet and used as a quiz or as a study aid for a test. In an analysis of past graphic organizer research, Moore and Readence (1984) found it advantageous to ask students to construct graphic organizers after reading, especially when vocabulary words were used in the graphic. This lends support to the practice of using graphic organizers as a postreading activity.

Fading from teacher to student control is difficult with the graphic organizer since prior knowledge of the topic is necessary. It would be quite easy for a teacher to model the use of a graphic organizer, but guided practice and independent use would be more difficult. If extended into a reading and postreading activity, fading can be accomplished as students become familiar with text patterns and the graphic organizer. After the teacher introduces the concept of graphic organizers and students master the skills necessary for their construction, students can be encouraged to survey text chapters independently and produce original diagrams. These rough graphic organizers can be refined by students as they read by adding, deleting, or modifying the original diagrams. The diagrams can be compared in small groups, with students defending their reasoning for choices made. Students can use the modified versions of their graphic organizers as study guides. Again, caution students that there is no correct construction as long as the graphic organizer adequately depicts the development and relationships between major concepts.

## Outline

Outlining skills have been taught for years. The outline is similar to the web and the graphic organizer in that major concepts and pertinent details are identified; the difference is in how the information is graphically represented. In the web, information radiates in spokes outward from the major topic. The graphic organizer presents coordinate terms in a parallel structure. In the outline, information is hierarchically organized. This strategy is often used with content material to impose a written structure on term papers, to organize class lecture notes, and as a means to study for a test.

Research indicates that outlines presented before a reading task facilitate student comprehension. Glynn and DiVesta (1977) found that factual recall was significantly improved when outlines were used as a prereading technique to familiarize students with new material. In an earlier study, Proger et al. (1970) found that using sentence outlines as prereading strategies enhanced the retention of specific conceptual information. Outlining can be an efficient vehicle for promoting learning when used before the information is presented in text and when teachers maintain responsibility for its construction.

An example of an outline which could be used for the topic on fibers might look like the following.

Fibers
I. Natural
   A. Vegetable
      1. Cotton
      2. Linen
   B. Animal
      1. Wool
      2. Silk

II. Man made
   A. Chemical
      1. Acrylic
      2. Rayon
      3. Nylon
      4. Polyester
      5. Acetate

In presenting the outline to a class, the teacher could use an overhead projector with a sheet of paper as a mask. As each new element of the outline is uncovered, the teacher should clarify unclear points and encourage discussion to assess prior knowledge. The organization of the text will become apparent through the gradual building of the text structure in outline form.

The use of outlines should be restricted to texts arranged in an ordered format where general concepts are sequentially introduced and supported with appropriate detail. Texts that do not follow such an organized format would be poor candidates for this strategy. When the text is loosely organized, a graphic organizer probably would be more useful.

An incomplete diagram can be used with the outline, with students relying on headings and subheadings in the text to fill in the incomplete form. Students follow the sequential development of the text to decide which terms fit the blanks. Unlike the graphic organizer, only a limited number of terms properly fit each blank because of the more organized text format.

In fading outlining instruction, it is important that the concept of outlining be understood before independent practice takes place (Hofler, 1983). Many students successfully complete outline workbook exercises without really understanding what an outline is. Identifying main idea, topic and subtopic, and details and subdetails is crucial to fading instruction, as is the ability to identify texts that do not lend themselves to the outline format. Students must realize that outlining cannot be done effectively with all texts. Through modeling, teachers can provide examples to students based on information being studied.

## Word Map

A word map is a graphic representation of the definition of a word (Pearson & Johnson, 1978). It is based on the notion that before students can say what a word means, they must have developed a concept of *definition* (Schwartz & Raphael, 1985). They must have the ability to identify and define new terms on their own, using prior knowledge and context clues. This strategy is ideal for moving students away from traditional teacher directed vocabulary lessons toward independence. It is useful in all content areas for students at all levels of instruction.

In traditional vocabulary instruction from basal and content texts, when students are told to use the context to figure out the meaning of an unknown word, they often do not understand exactly what is meant. They may understand that context means the surrounding words and sentences without knowing exactly where they can find the information they need, since each example is unique. Often students do not realize that they have prior knowledge which may help them define an unknown word.

Schwartz and Raphael (1985) outlined the steps needed to teach students how to use word maps to define unknown words. Three categories of word relation-

Word Map for Bear

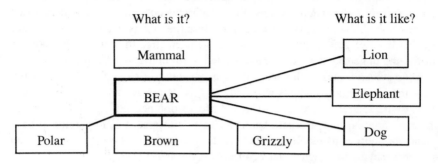

What are some examples?

ships are used in word maps: (1) the general class to which a word belongs (What is it?); (2) the important properties of the word including those that distinguish it from members of its class (What is it like?); and (3) examples of the concept (What are some examples?). Word maps usually work better with nouns, but can be used with action verbs and other parts of speech. An example of a word map structure is shown.

In the center of the map, in the largest square, the concept being studied is written. Then, a general word or short phrase, describing what the word is, is written in the square at the top. This word is often the name of a generic class to which the word belongs. For instance, if *bear* is the concept being studied, a good word for the top square would be *mammal.* Next, the student answers the question, "What is it like?" with words that fit the same category as the center word; for example, *lion, elephant,* and *dog.* It is important for these words to be at the same level as the word being studied. For example, *animal* would be a poor choice because it is a broader term than bear. *Dalmatian* would be a poor choice since it is a specific breed of dog and not a generic mammal. Examples of the concept are written in the bottom squares. *Polar, brown,* and *grizzly* are examples of bears.

Begin teaching word mapping to students by direct instruction through modeling. Students should learn the importance of figuring out unknown words while reading. Teachers can provide students with the motivation and enthusiasm for wanting to learn the meanings of new words. A strategy such as Contextual Redefinition (outlined in Chapter 4) can lead students into a discussion of the importance of knowing methods for gaining new word meanings. The word map form can be shown on an overhead transparency or chalkboard, and concepts known to students can be mapped. By using familiar examples, students gain valuable practice in understanding the categories of questions used.

After students are familiar with the general format of word maps, the teacher can construct independent exercises in which concepts are introduced in a rich context and all the information needed to fill in the map is in the text being read. At this level of guided practice, students gain practice in identifying unknown words and in getting the information needed to fill in the map form from context.

After students master this step, the teacher can use examples that gradually limit the information students will find. At this step, students should be encouraged to use reference materials to locate information needed. Encyclopedias, almanacs, atlases, and alternate texts can help students. It is important to have plenty of sources available for students to use in the classroom, since several students may be looking up word concepts at the same time.

Fading instruction is complete when students can internalize the questions from the word map, giving definitions of words without going through the mapping procedure. As students come across important unfamiliar terms while reading independently, they should ask themselves, "What is this word? What is it like? What are some examples of the word?" Students can revert to using the map individually, if needed, on words particularly difficult to understand.

Word maps have two advantages over some other methods of teaching students to understand the meanings of unknown words and concepts. First, by using the mapping technique (whether physically mapping the word or internally questioning about the word), students gain more exposure to the word than simply looking up the meaning in the dictionary. This increases the chances that the word will be identified and defined at a later date. Second, word mapping promotes independent learning. The concept of fading instruction is built in, as the teacher instructs, provides examples, and practices the strategy with students. The steps in mapping are clear, and hopefully will eliminate the uncertainty many students have during vocabulary instruction related to basal and content text.

## Summary

This chapter has presented a rationale for graphically representing information in order to maximize student interaction with text. Several strategies have been presented which allow teachers to provide students with the tools for enhancing comprehension and promoting independent learning. These strategies can be used effectively before and after reading to allow students to organize the information for reading and/or study. Suggestions for fading instructional support from teacher to student control have been discussed.

### References
Barron, R.F., and Earle, R.A. An approach for vocabulary instruction. In H.L. Herber and R.F. Barron (Eds.), *Research in reading in the content areas: Second year report.* Syracuse, NY: Syracuse University Reading and Language Arts Center, 1973, 84-100.

　　　　　　　　　　　　　　　　　　　　　　　Prereading Activities

Beck, I.L., Omanson, R.C., and McKeown, M.G. An instructional redesign of reading lessons: Effects on comprehension. *Reading Research Quarterly,* 1982, *17,* 462-481.

Boothby, P.R., and Alvermann, D.E. A classroom training study: The effects of graphic organizer instruction on fourth graders' comprehension. *Reading World,* 1984, *23,* 325-339.

Clewell, S.F., and Haldemos, J. Organizational strategies to increase comprehension. *Reading World,* 1983, *22,* 314-321.

DiVesta, F.J., Schultz, C.B., and Dangel, T.R. Passage organization and imposed learning strategies in comprehension and recall of connected discourse. *Memory and Cognition,* 1973, *1,* 471-476.

Draper, W., and Bailey, A. *Steps in clothing skills,* revised edition. Peoria, IL: Charles A. Bennet, 1978.

Earle, R.A. *Teaching reading and mathematics.* Newark, DE: International Reading Association, 1976.

Glynn, S.M., and DiVesta, F.J. Outline and hierarchical organization as aids for study and retrieval. *Journal of Educational Psychology,* 1977, *69,* 89-95.

Hofler, D.B. Outlining: Teach the concept first. *Reading World,* 1983, *23,* 176-177.

Lunstrum, J.P., and Taylor, B.L. *Teaching reading in the social studies.* Newark, DE: International Reading Association, 1978.

Moore, D.W., and Readence, J.E. A quantitative and qualitative review of graphic organizer research. *Journal of Educational Research,* 1984, *78,* 11-17.

Pearson, P.D., and Johnson, D.D. *Teaching reading comprehension.* New York: Holt, Rinehart & Winston, 1978.

Proger, B.B., Taylor, R.G., Mann, L., Coulson, J.M., and Bayuk, R.J. Conceptual prestructuring for detailed verbal passages. *Journal of Educational Research,* 1970, *64,* 28-34.

Readence, J.E., Bean, T.W., and Baldwin, R.S. *Content area reading: An integrated approach,* second edition. Dubuque, IA: Kendall/Hunt, 1985.

Readence, J.E., and Moore, D.W. Strategies for enhancing readiness and recall in content areas: The encoding specificity principle. *Reading Psychology,* 1979, *1,* 47-54.

Reutzel, D.R. Story maps improve comprehension. *The Reading Teacher,* 1985, *38,* 400-404.

Rumelhart, D.E., and Ortony, A. The representation of knowledge in memory. In R.C. Anderson, R.J. Spiro, and W.E. Montague (Eds.), *Schooling and the acquisition of knowledge.* Hillsdale, NJ: Erlbaum, 1977, 99-135.

Schwartz, R.M., and Raphael, T.E. Concept of definition: A key to improving students' vocabulary. *The Reading Teacher,* 1985, *39,* 198-205.

Sinatra, R.C., Stahl-Gemake, J., and Berg, D.N. Improving reading comprehension of disabled readers through semantic mapping. *The Reading Teacher,* 1984, *38,* 22-29.

Smith, C.F. *The structured overview: Theory and practice.* Madison, WI: Wisconsin Department of Public Instruction, 1979.

Thelen, J. *Improving reading in science,* second edition. Newark, DE: International Reading Association, 1984.

Tierney, R.J., Readence, J.E., and Dishner, E.K. *Reading strategies and practices: A compendium,* second edition. Boston: Allyn & Bacon, 1985.

van Dijk, T.A., and Kintsch, W. *Strategies of discourse comprehension.* New York: Academic Press, 1983.

Chapter 6

# Writing before Reading

| **Purpose** | *Writing before and after reading promotes learning in a manner similar to the other strategies presented in this monograph. A special value of writing is that it provides a permanent record of thoughts.* |
|---|---|

**Strategies**
1. *Identification with a Story Character* begins with students writing about a situation similar to one a story character experiences.
2. The *Guided Writing Procedure* calls for students to brainstorm and categorize words related to a topic of study, use those words when writing about the topic, and then read a related passage.
3. The *Hennings Sequence* prepares students for writing in a manner similar to the Guided Writing Procedure, but the Hennings Sequence details additional ways to help students draft the information they generate.
4. *Free Writing* involves stream of consciousness recording of what students know about a topic.

---

**W**riting about a topic provides students opportunities to enhance their learning. Students who record their thoughts on paper frequently gain understandings that might be missed and retain understandings that might be forgotten. The effect of writing on learning received unprecedented attention by researchers and theorists during the 1970s and early 1980s (Applebee, 1984), and much was published about writing in the content areas (Fulwiler & Young, 1982; Martin, 1976; Mayher, Lester, & Pradl, 1983).

The emphasis in this chapter differs from the emphases of most books and articles on writing. Here we focus on writing as a prereading strategy, with emphasis on increasing students' learning from text. We suggest having students write what they know about a topic before reading about it to maximize reading comprehension and retention.

The general rationale of writing before reading matches the rationale of the other prereading strategies presented in this monograph. Writing before reading is especially useful for increasing motivation by stimulating students' curiosity, activating students' prior knowledge, and focusing students' attention on important information.

Along with these outcomes, writing seems to improve learning from text because it provides a permanent record of thoughts (Emig, 1977; Odell, 1980). Writers use the permanence of paper, chalkboards, and computers to hold their words in place. With a record of their thoughts permanently stored, writers are able to examine and refine their thinking. Careful review and revision of one's thoughts are possible when a written record is available.

The permanence of writing can be exploited before reading so that learners produce a complete, well defined statement of what they do and do not know about a topic, thereby enhancing readiness for reading. Of equal importance, learners can write about a topic, read about it, and then return to their original statement in order to apply what they just learned and to revise the original. Documenting intellectual growth this way seems to improve learning.

## A Brief Retrospective

This chapter on writing before reading is deliberately located at the end of the book. The reason for placing this chapter after the ones on asking and answering questions, forecasting passages, understanding vocabulary, and graphically representing information is to point out that many of the teaching strategies already presented could involve writing. Students could participate orally in ReQuest, the Directed Reading-Thinking Activity, the Anticipation Guide, and Contextual Redefinition, or they could participate through writing. This chapter describes additional ways to capitalize on the power of writing before reading.

## Writing Tasks

Tasks are the assigned work students are expected to complete; tasks are the basic units of instruction teachers manipulate as they move through the school day (Doyle, 1983). The following illustrates different types of writing tasks that might be assigned before having students read.

- Teacher A displays key words from a unit on Brazil and asks students to write an essay that includes all the words. The students then read about Brazil, check their essays for accuracy, and modify them if necessary.
- Teacher B asks students to brainstorm what should be included in a brochure

they will produce promoting Brazil to potential tourists. After the brainstorming session, students read in order to determine what else their brochures should include.

- Teacher C asks students to write what they think they would like best about visiting Brazil. The students then read about Brazil.
- Teacher D gives students five minutes to write whatever they want about Brazil. The students then read about this country.

The assignments of teachers A through D illustrate three distinguishing features of writing tasks. These features can be classified on continuums of directed/free, personal/impersonal, and conventional/enriched. Figure 1 displays a feature matrix of the types of tasks assigned by Teachers A through D.

Figure 1
Feature Matrix of Representative Teachers'
Types of Writing Tasks

| Teacher | Direct | Free | Impersonal | Personal | Conventional | Enriched |
|---------|--------|------|------------|----------|--------------|----------|
| A | + | – | + | – | + | – |
| B | + | – | + | – | – | + |
| C | + | – | – | + | + | – |
| D | – | + | +/– | +/– | +/– | +/– |

## Directed/Free Writing

As Figure 1 shows, Teachers A, B, and C provide directed tasks; they order a particular type of writing from their students each time a writing task is assigned. Conversely, Teacher D offers free writing tasks. This teacher expects his or her students to write about a certain topic, but the exact nature of the task is left up to the individual. Some authorities might argue that defining the topic for students makes the writing task directed, but here it is considered free if that is all the teacher does before offering individual assistance.

## Personal/Impersonal Writing

The writing tasks of Teachers A, B, and C can be classified on a personal/impersonal continuum. (Teacher D cannot be classified on this continuum because his or her students decide what to write, and their choices will vary.) Teacher C assigns personal tasks; they relate what is being studied to students' lives. Teacher C asks students to describe what they would like about Brazil. Students' feelings are elicited and applied to the topic of study. Personal writing tasks connect students' own experiences, beliefs, and feelings with the topic being studied. On the other hand, Teachers A and B assign impersonal tasks. These assignments do not connect the subject matter directly with students' lives. Although impersonal tasks might have students call up what they know about a topic, these tasks ignore the actual experiences and reactions individuals have relative to the topic.

## Conventional/Enriched Writing

Finally, Teachers A and B assign tasks that differ on the conventional/enriched continuum. (Teacher D cannot be classified on this continuum either because some students might choose conventional writing and some might choose enriched writing.) Teacher A presents conventional tasks. Teacher A has students write traditional papers that are found mainly in school settings. The conventional tasks of Teacher A emphasize academic concerns and bear little relation to the writing done outside of school. In contrast, Teacher B provides students with tasks that are enriched, that have practical significance. Teacher B always designates a relevant writing form (e.g., a brochure) and an audience (e.g., potential tourists to Brazil).

## A Final Word

Given the possible types of writing tasks presented by Teachers A, B, C, and D, which are best? On which end of the continuums should writing before reading tasks lie? Should they be directed or free, enriched or conventional, personal or impersonal?

A balanced program of writing before reading tasks seems most desirable. Directed writing contributes to learning, but students also should engage in free writing to enhance their learning from text. In addition, conventional and enriched tasks have merits relative to each. Summarizing a passage seems to be as important as retelling a passage in a letter to a friend. Personal and impersonal writing also deserve attention. Connecting personal experiences and values to a topic seems as important as maintaining an objective impersonal stance about a topic. To repeat, a balanced program of tasks seems most appropriate for learning from text.

## Writing Lessons

Designing tasks is only part of the strategy of using writing to enhance reading. Tasks define what the finished product is to be, but do not specify the process students are to follow. In other words, telling students to produce a brochure about Brazil differs from teaching students how to produce such a brochure. Teaching students how to complete tasks is another dimension of instruction. This section emphasizes four writing strategies and describes how teachers and students can work together to complete certain tasks.

## Identification with a Story Character

Marino, Gould, and Haas (1985) reported the benefits of having students identify with a story character through writing before reading about the character. Their writing before reading task was directed, enriched, and personal. The task follows.

> Pretend you are a young person in 1845. You are a pioneer heading for the Oregon country. You and your family have stopped to make camp for the night on the Snake River when you meet a group of young orphans. The oldest is a 13 year old boy who tells you of his determination to carry on with his father's plans to take the family to Oregon. John, you learn, is a very brave and clever boy who has just saved his sister from drowning. Write a letter home to your grandparents describing this boy and the story he has told you (p.204).

Note that this task was directed (teacher prescribed what was to be written), contained a relevant form (letter), an audience (your grandparents), and was personal (pretend you are a young person).

The experimental group consisted of thirty fourth grade students. They were given thirty minutes to write, and, immediately after writing, they were given thirty minutes to read the 2,000 word passage about Oregon from which the writing task was derived. Before reading the passage about Oregon, the thiry control group students wrote about an interesting event that actually happened to them. A written recall test of the Oregon story was given the next day.

The experimental subjects recalled more about the passage than the control subjects, and low achieving readers seemed to perform especially well with the treatment. As the researchers explained, their results seemed to occur partly as a function of the personal nature of the task. Students responded affectively to the character, John; many students wrote about sharing fictitious events and a close friendship with him. Emotionally identifying with the character in the story before reading seemed to promote comprehension. In addition, the researchers attributed part of the benefit of their task to the audience that was specified. Writing to an audience such as grandparents (even if they are pretend) seemed to enhance the task.

To summarize, Identification with a Story Character, as presented by Marino, Gould, and Haas (1985), consists of three steps.

1. Design a task that elicits identification with a story character.
2. Have students write in response to the task.
3. Have students read the passage from which the task was derived.

## Guided Writing Procedure

The Guided Writing Procedure (GWP) (Smith & Bean, 1980) was designed in part to help students synthesize and retain content area material. The two day procedure that follows is a slight adaptation of the original GWP description.

1. Have students brainstorm what they know about an upcoming topic of study (volcanoes) and record their responses on a chalkboard or overhead transparency. A possible list follows.

*Volcanoes*

| | |
|---|---|
| lava | Mt. St. Helens |
| destruction | eruption |
| ashes | crater |
| hot | dangerous |
| steam | fiery |

2. Identify categories that encompass the brainstormed terms (physical qualities, descriptions, examples) and list details that support the category titles.
3. Represent the category titles and their details in forms such as an outline, web, or graphic organizer.

   I. Physical Qualities
   A. Crater
   B. Eruption
      1. lava
      2. ashes
      3. steam
   II. Description
   A. Fiery
      1. hot
   B. Dangerous
      1. destruction
   III. Example
   A. Mt. St. Helens

4. Have students write about the topic, using the graphically presented information.
5. Have students read a passage related to the topic of study to determine how their papers could be expanded or modified. For example, students might search for additional information about the physical qualities of volcanoes.

As can be seen, the first three GWP steps in Day One merge List-Group-Label with the procedures for graphically representing information presented earlier in this monograph. The Day One GWP steps neatly connect these strategies before writing and reading.

*Day Two*

1. Display a few students' papers with an overhead projector. Examples of good and poor writing should be demonstrated, and they might be selected from students not currently in class in order to avoid embarrassment. Revise the papers according to content as well as two or three writing criteria. (See Figure 2 for a list of possible criteria.)

Figure 2
Possible Writing Criteria

| | High | | | Low |
|---|---|---|---|---|
| • Passage Organization | | | | |
| *Informational Writing* | | | | |
| Major and minor points are distinguishable; topic sentence(s) stated and supported with relevant details. | 4 | 3 | 2 | 1 |
| *Narrative Stories* | | | | |
| Story plot has identifiable beginning, middle, and end with characters introduced, a problem, and a believable or logical solution. | 4 | 3 | 2 | 1 |
| • Engagement | | | | |
| The paper grasps the reader's attention by presenting vivid language in imaginative, effective ways; words are included that sharply and clearly define ideas. | 4 | 3 | 2 | 1 |
| • Sentence Structure | | | | |
| Sentences are well formed, complete thoughts with no run ons. | 4 | 3 | 2 | 1 |
| • Spelling | | | | |
| All familiar words are spelled correctly; any misspellings of unfamiliar words are quite close to the correct form. | 4 | 3 | 2 | 1 |

2. Have students revise their papers according to the content and writing criteria just demonstrated. Teachers frequently have students evaluate a partner's composition before having them rewrite.

The GWP has some research support for its effectiveness in enhancing learning from text (Konopak, Martin, & Martin, 1987; Martin & Konopak, 1987; Martin, Konopak, & Martin, 1986). For example, Martin, Konopak, and Martin reported that high school juniors reading a 500 word passage on the California Gold Rush benefited from the GWP when compared with control group students who read the passage and completed word identification and short answer comprehension tasks. In particular, the GWP students produced higher order concepts more frequently than the control group, and they synthesized information from their brainstorming session and from their reading.

It is important to realize that the results obtained by the studies reported here will not necessarily occur with other students reading other passages in other situations. The circumstances present during the studies by Marino, Gould, and Haas (1985) and Martin, Konopak, and Martin (1986) probably will not be present when other educators try the teaching strategies. Perhaps the greatest value of this research is its clear illustration of specific ways that writing before reading benefited particular students' learning from text. Educators can use these studies to suggest—not guarantee—ways that writing might influence learning.

## Hennings Sequence

Hennings (1982) described a sequence of steps designed to clarify the organization of informational content. The Hennings Sequence (we coined the label) is intended for elementary school children, although it can be adapted for all grade levels. It synthesizes much of the current thinking about helping students organize factual information. Hennings presented her sequence as a way to prepare students for reading informational text, although many of the eight steps will be familiar to those who have guided students through research reports.

1. *Factstorming.* Students first become familiar with a topic through viewing filmstrips, films, and slides; interviewing people; going on excursions; reading; talking; and doing and observing. Students then brainstorm what they know about the topic, calling out information for someone to record on a chalkboard.

2. *Categorizing facts.* Students next organize the terms randomly produced during the first step. The categories can be determined and recorded several ways. One way is to circle a word with a colored marker and circle related words with the same color. Another way is to produce a data chart. Data charts consist of a grid with headings always over the columns and occasionally beside the rows. The students or the teacher may provide the headings, and the headings may be given before or after factstorming. Data chart cells are filled by students on their own or by teachers with student input. Factstormed information should be included, and students might consult reading materials, adults, and other sources of information in order to fill the cells with facts. Intermediate students might employ the Data Chart for Tigers displayed in Figure 3. A high school natural science class might use the Data Chart for Flowering Plants shown in Figure 4.

Figure 3

Data Chart for Tigers

| Where do tigers live? | What do tigers eat? | What dangers do tigers face? |
|---|---|---|
|  |  |  |

### Figure 4

#### Data Chart for Flowering Plants

| | Herbaceous Dicot | Woody Dicot | Herbaceous Monocot | Woody Monocot |
|---|---|---|---|---|
| Common Types | | | | |
| Internal Stem Structure | | | | |
| External Stem Structure | | | | |

3. *Drafting cohesive paragraphs.* Once information is categorized, students draft paragraphs. Hennings recommends that students share the work by having groups take responsibility for certain categories of information. If a data chart were used, then students could be directed to translate into a paragraph the information contained in a column, row, or cell.

4. *Sequencing paragraphs into a logical whole.* Students share their paragraphs and decide on the best order for the final report. A data chart would be helpful in framing the order of paragraphs.

5. *Drafting introductions and conclusions.* The introduction and conclusion of a paper seem to come more readily after, rather than before, the contents of a report are written. To write an introduction and a conclusion, you need to know what you are introducing and concluding. Hennings suggests composing the beginning and ending of a paper as a teacher guided group writing activity.

6. *Organizing the parts into a cohesive report.* A few students put together a final draft of the paper. A main title and subheadings for each of the categories should be included.

7. *Interpreting similar pieces of discourse.* Students who have gone through the first six steps of the Hennings Sequence probably understand the struc-

ture of informational content better than students who only have read such material. Writers seem to have an advantage over those who only read because writers realize how passages are put together.

Taking what students have learned about the structure of materials, teachers guide students to find the same structures in what they read. For instance, students can use a data chart to recover essential information from new passages. At this point, data charts become tools for postreading rather than prewriting.

    8. *Summarizing, synthesizing, and judging.* The final step calls for students to return to writing, only this time the writing is based directly on information obtained through reading. In the case of the data chart in Figure 4, students might be asked to read a new passage about plants and summarize the internal and external structure of woody dicots, explain the differences between herbaceous monocots and herbaceous dicots, or judge which plant is most helpful to humans. These new tasks illustrate the give and take between comprehending and composing.

The Hennings Sequence collapses some steps of the writing before reading process that the GWP separates, but Hennings also separates some steps that the GWP collapses. For instances, the GWP step four (have students write about the topic) is separated into steps three, four, five, and six by Hennings. When taken together, these strategies offer a complete view of a writing before reading procedure.

## Free Writing

Free writing gained popularity in the 1970s as a way to release students who had difficulty getting the writing act started. Authorities such as Elbow (1973) and Macrorie (1976) tout free writing as a way to loosen writers and get their ideas flowing.

The important thing in free writing is to continually produce words. Students do not need to worry about written mechanics or structure as they write thoughts in whatever order they come. The standard recommendation for students who complain "I don't know what to write" is to have them copy "I don't know what to write" until some thoughts occur. One way to stimulate free writing is to play music and have students write whatever occurs to them while listening. This strategy is a nonthreatening way to help students record their thoughts fluently.

Free writing can be used for preparing students to learn from text. It is the strategy Teacher D used (e.g., For the next five minutes, write whatever you want about Brazil). Although free writing typically calls for students to originate their own topics, one variation is to assign a topic and have students write freely about it for a certain period of time (Kirby & Liner, 1981). Free writing is similar to brainstorming because students recall and record information according to whatever associations occur to them (Murray, 1984). This strategy can be motivating and informative for students who are preparing to study.

Having students maintain content journals is a good way to foster free writing. Content journals, also called academic journals (Fulwiler, 1980) or learning logs (Sanders, 1985), are appropriate for all school subjects. Students record in a notebook their insights about the topics being studied in class. Fulwiler describes content journals as a cross between diaries and class notes. They are like diaries because they contain personal thoughts and like class notes because they focus on subject matter information.

Having students write freely in their journals before reading can be accomplished several ways. Many teachers provide five or ten minutes of class time each day for students to record their journal entries. When a prereading strategy is appropriate, teachers might have students write in their journals at the beginning of the class. Teachers might list key words from an upcoming chapter and have students write freely about them as prereading preparation. Questions might be asked such as, "How well can I explain these concepts?" "How much can I say about them?" "What do I know or not know about this topic?" Students can share what they write if they wish. Students date each entry and maintain a table of contents.

## Direct Instruction with Writing before Reading

The goal of having students independently write before they read can be met through direct instruction. To illustrate, one of the basic components of the GWP and the Hennings Sequence, brainstorming information, can be faded from a teacher directed to a student directed process.

## Demonstration

Begin the demonstration stage by labeling the strategy. Tell students that writing before reading is one way to improve learning, and brainstorming is an important part of this. Briefly define brainstorming and explain its relevance. Depending on the age and maturity of the students, specify actual instances in the present and future when brainstorming would be appropriate as a part of writing before reading.

The next step is to model the strategy, which frequently can be done in a few minutes. For instance, if you want your students to brainstorm what they know about a topic, you might say, "Give me a topic, and watch how I brainstorm what I know about it." After brainstorming for awhile, stop and explain what you just did. Articulate how to use the strategy: "Did you notice how I wrote very quickly as I called out what I knew? And did you see how quickly I worked? You should think and write quickly when you brainstorm."

## d Practice

nonstrating what you want your students to do, give them a chance to time they try the strategy might be as a large group: "Now it's your turn, class. Here's the topic, so call out everything you know about it just as I did." Several students might record words the class calls out. Provide feedback about their performance: "Good, you're moving quickly. Keep the words coming, we'll work with them later."

Teachers frequently have students work in pairs or small groups during the guided practice stage. Working together, students share insights about the process and jointly solve problems. Guided practice with feedback should continue until students seem adept with the strategy.

## Independent Application

In order to foster independent application, have students use the strategy once they are skillful with it: "This passage contains vital information. If you understand its key points, you'll understand the fundamental concepts we'll be covering the next four weeks. Therefore, take some time and write what you know about this topic before reading." Assistance then can be provided as needed.

It is important to realize that independent application is meant to prompt students to do what they have been previously taught. Simply telling students to write before they read without demonstrating the strategy and providing guided practice defies the tenets of direct, explicit instruction.

## Summary

The rationale of writing before reading as an aid to learning is similar to the rationale of the other prereading strategies presented in this monograph. The fact that writing provides a permanent record of thoughts is an additional benefit. Writing tasks can be classified on continuums of directed/free, personal/impersonal, and conventional/enriched. A balanced program of writing tasks seems most appropriate for enhancing learning from text. Four strategies for helping students complete writing before reading tasks and promote learning are Identification with a Story Character, the Guided Writing Procedure, the Hennings Sequence, and Free Writing. The brainstorming component of these strategies can be taught readily through a program of direct instruction.

### References

Applebee, A.N. Writing and reasoning. *Review of Educational Research,* 1984, *54,* 577-596.

Doyle, W. Academic work. *Review of Educational Research,* 1983, *53,* 159-199.

Elbow, P. *Writing without teachers.* New York: Oxford University Press, 1973.

Emig, J. Writing as a mode of learning. *College Composition and Communication,* 1977, *28,* 122-127.

Fulwiler, T. Journals across the disciplines. *English Journal,* 1980, *69,* 14-19.

Fulwiler, T., and Young, A. (Eds.). *Language connections: Writing and reading across the curriculum.* Urbana, IL: National Council of Teachers of English, 1982.

Hennings, D.G. A writing approach to reading comprehension: Schema theory in action. *Language Arts,* 1982, *59,* 8-17.

Kirby, D., and Liner, T. *Inside out: Developmental strategies for teaching writing.* Upper Montclair, NJ: Boynton/Cook, 1981.

Konopak, B.C., Martin, S.H., and Martin, M.A. An integrated communications arts approach for enhancing students' learning in content areas. *Reading Research and Instruction,* 1987, *26,* 275-289.

Macrorie, K. *Writing to be read,* second edition. Rochelle Park, NJ: Hayden, 1976.

Marino, J.L., Gould, S.M., and Haas, L.W. The effects of writing as a prereading activity on delayed recall of narrative text. *Elementary School Journal,* 1985, *86,* 199-205.

Martin, M.A., Konopak, B.C., and Martin, S.H. Use of the guided writing procedure to facilitate comprehension of high school text materials. In J.A. Niles and R.V. Lalik (Eds.), *Solving problems in literacy: Learners, teachers, and researchers.* Thirty-Fifth Yearbook of the National Reading Conference. Rochester, NY: National Reading Conference, 1986, 66-72.

Martin, M.A., and Konopak, B.C. An instructional investigation of students' ideas generated during content area writing. In J.E. Readence and R.E. Baldwin (Eds.), *Research in literacy: Merging perspectives.* Thirty-Sixth Yearbook of the National Reading Conference, 1987, 265-271.

Martin, N. *Writing and learning across the curriculum.* London: Ward Lock Educational, 1976.

Mayher, J.S., Lester, N.B., and Pradl, G.M. *Learning to write/Writing to learn.* Upper Montclair, NJ: Boynton/Cook, 1983.

Murray, D. *Write to learn.* New York: Holt, Rinehart & Winston, 1984.

Odell, L. The process of writing and the process of learning. *College Composition and Communication,* 1980, *21,* 42-50.

Sanders, A. Learning logs: A communication strategy for all subject areas. *Educational Leadership,* 1985, *42,* 7.

Smith, C.C., and Bean, T.W. The guided writing procedure: Integrating content reading and writing improvement, *Reading World,* 1980, *19,* 290-294.